Smith would like to dedicate her portion of this book to BBC iPlayer, Audible, and Netflix. I genuinely do not think I could have done it without you.

Jones dedicates her offering to her mother for introducing her to yarn and needles all those years ago, supporting her first baby steps on this journey, and bestowing such a wonderful gift - the joy that comes from 'making stuff'.

First published in 2015 by Smith & Jones Knits.

Copyright © Smith & Jones Knits 2015
Designs and Patterns by Alison Crowther-Smith
copyright
© Alison Crowther-Smith 2015
Designs and Patterns by Donna Jones copyright
© Donna Jones 2015

Created and Produced by Smith & Jones Knits
10 Devonshire Place
Port Talbot
SA13 1SG

Photography: Smith & Jones Knits
Styling: Smith & Jones Knits
Technical Editing: Donna Jones
Pattern Checking and technical advice: Sarah Hatton
Layout Design: Emma Chapman

British Library Cataloguing in Publication Data
A catalogue record of this book is available from
the British Library

ISBN 978-0-9932326-0-2

Printed in the UK by Lion FPG Limited

CONTENTS

DESIGNS

'Elements' is a collaborative knitting collection. The concept is simple. Each designer has created a collection drawn from her own native landscape. For Alison this is the hills, levels and gardens of Somerset, whilst for Donna it is the forests, coasts and home-lands of South Wales. Together, they make up 'Elements'.

Whilst the design inspirations and styles of the authors are very different, they are also highly complementary. 'Elements' will take you on a journey through a year in the British landscapes where the authors live and work, echoing the English and Welsh land and seascapes where each designer finds herself to be in her element. This collection captures the elements of weather and seasons, but at its heart it is close to home, drawing you into the comfort of home and garden throughout the year.

The designs range in complexity, from straightforward easy knitting to projects that offer more of a challenge, and are suitable for knitters with basic to more advanced levels of expertise. Those wishing to develop their abilities further will benefit from the full colour photograph technique section, in which the designers clearly show you how to develop new skills.

Knitted in beautiful Rowan yarns, 'Elements' includes 24 hand knit designs, including accessories, garments and home-wares. Both designers are passionate about using colour, albeit in very different ways, and both have included some of their favourite knitting styles and techniques, such as Fairisle, intarsia, beads, lace and texture. 'Elements' is a striking collection, moving from beautiful folk-art inspired comfort, to spare and elegant style as the two designers lead you into their creative worlds. And finally, it is a true example of the whole definitely being greater than the sum of its parts: two designers in one inspiring book.

DRIFT FOLDED SHRUG

This shrug, like the Drift Mittens (page 18), uses a folded stitch detail to give me the fabric design I wanted: deep undulations, suggestive of a landscape that is very dear to me, the Mendip Hills in Somerset. I chose a spare, classic dove-grey. The bleached winter grass often turns a silvery grey colour up on these hills. Below this folded contour is another Mendip world. The caves that lie below are deep and full of a beauty all their own.

Pattern on page **60**

ICE BOA
IN COCOON

Whilst its glamorous sister, the beaded Ice Boa knitted in
Kidsilk Haze and **Fine Lace**, is more at home with chic,
city winter style, this boa by contrast is a chunky and
simplified version. The deep godet-style double 'inserts',
when knitted in **Cocoon,** have fantastic visual impact
and create a swirling water-fall edge effect. This is your
practical Ice Boa, ideal for winter dog-walking days.
Pattern on page **62**

RIME
FAIRISLE SNOOD

Knitted in the round, this shrug can be pulled down over the shoulders as a stylish seamless wrap, worn more loosely at the neck, or snugly pulled up and over the head, as a snood. My inspiration for this piece is the simple and gradual shift of winter from the depths of November to the longer days and wider skies of February. Almost imperceptible at the time, suddenly you find yourself in the light of broadening spring.

Pattern on page **64**

ICE BOA

An unapologetic confection of frills and beads. The construction is simple enough – lace-sided, beaded godets or inserts are knitted to form a series of flowing frills. Once this pattern is established, we add further inserts, a lacy cast off and a delicate top frill.

Its creamy fabric, which is knitted with **Kidsilk Haze** and **Fine Lace** held together is really delicate; the crystal beads add subtle ice to this snowy boa.

Pattern on page **66**

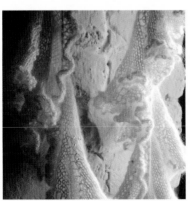

ICE CUFFS

Cuffs may seem to some people – not us, of course – to be rather impractical. I am not going to suggest that you'd wear these to prune the roses. However, they do keep you quite snug whilst at the same time making you feel amazingly glamorous. Peeping from the sleeve of your coat – or in the case of these cuffs, let's face it, actually showing off - you do really come over all Hollywood once you slip them on.

Pattern on page **68**

DRIFT FOLDED CUFF MITTS

These mittens and the companion piece shrug which uses the same folded stitch detail were the very first items I designed for this book. They remind me of the landscape of drifted snow which we always have at some time each winter up on the Mendips. Even when there is no snow, the contour of the Mendips, once you are on the very top, is folded, spare, and mysterious.

Pattern on page **70**

RISE SCARF

A mirror-image scarf – almost. On one side, the silver thread dominates, whilst on the other side, soft green woollen yarn eclipses the frost. Each year, I am amazed by the sturdiness of snow-drops as they push through crusted snow or frosted earth, granular from the repeated freeze and thaw. That is what I saw when I designed this scarf.

Pattern on page **72**

LANDSCAPE THROW

This very generous throw is both weighty and comforting. It grows
really fast in the beautifully soft, chunky **Cocoon** yarn.

The inspiration for me is the changing panorama of the Mendip
landscape, as winter ebbs into spring, whilst the constant thread of
its geography remains unchanged. Ideal for winter, this throw is also
a great comfort on those odd, chilly spring and summer evenings.

Pattern on page **74**

LANDSCAPE CUSHION

A companion piece to the Landscape Throw, this large cushion uses the same shades but the woven cable is extended to create the entire front, while the back has blocks of warm colour and over-sized buttons.
Pattern on page **76**

KITCHEN
GARDEN TUNIC

This cosy and practical tunic is for the most part knitted in simple
stocking stitch but has a couple of details which make for a bit
more of a challenge: a central inverted box pleat to the front and a
generous patch pocket.

Pattern on page **78**

GARDEN SONG BLANKET

A seemingly ambitious knit, this heirloom piece is knit in easily mánaged squares and then pieced together. Although beautifully cosy, the fine nature of **Felted Tweed** yields a surprising lightness to the blanket despite its generous size.

Pattern on page **81**

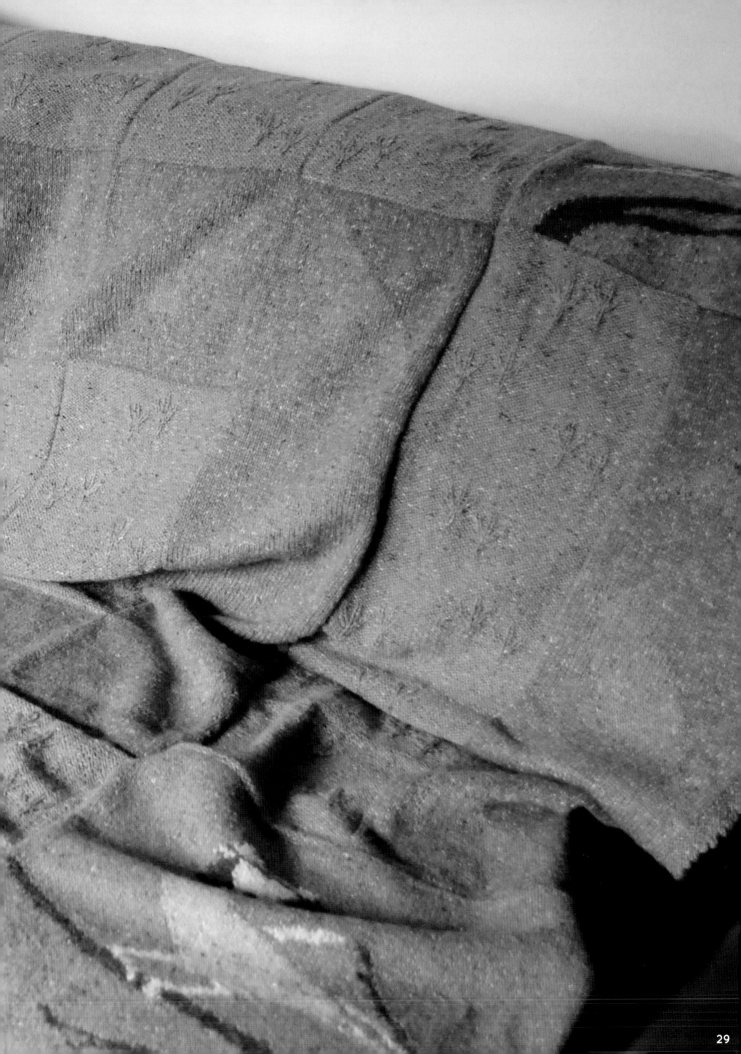

GARDEN SONG CUSHION

Bring the outdoors in with this delightful cushion inspired by
our little garden visitors. The cushion has a chirpy intarsia blue
tit at the front, with birdy footprint stitch detail to the back.
Pattern on page **87**

LUMI BEADED LACE MITTENS

These mittens are packed with styling features to make them elegant and pleasing to wear – and to knit. With deep cuffs, they will be snug and long enough to tuck into the sleeves of your coat, but they are also flared slightly at the very edge, so you can slip a fitted jumper-sleeve inside, if you prefer.

Pattern on page **89**

COCKLESHELL CARDIGAN

Knitted with **Panama** to produce a wonderfully light and summery cardigan with an elegant drape. With raglan sleeves and a gentle A line silhouette, Cockleshell will suit most body shapes and is sure to become a wardrobe workhorse.

Pattern on page **91**

COASTAL
BED RUNNER

Adorn your bed with a summery sea view; this beautifully
striped bed runner can also be worn as a stylish wrap
for sitting on the patio during the cooler ends of the day.
A relaxing knit that keeps your interest as you watch the
open sea emerge from your needles.

Pattern on page **94**

COASTAL CUSHION

Furnished with buttons made of Pembrokeshire Slate, the cushion front shares a sea view with the accompanying Coastal Runner, while inspiration has been drawn from rippled sand for the back.

Pattern on page **96**

BOREAL CAPELET

I really love capes and this is (so far) the closest I have got to knitting a proper 'fairy-tale' cloak.

This rich, velvety capelet is simply stitched, allowing the beautiful yarns to really excel. The main cape is knitted in chenille yarn, in plain stocking stitch, with careful, subtle tailoring to form the 'three-penny bit' shaped drape. The edge is then added: a gently fanned, pleated border in a cashmere blend yarn. The back of the neck is a soft arc of garter stitch.

Pattern on page **98**

NEST

This is a collection of three felted bowls and containers, each using a different technique or colour feature. None of the knitting is at all difficult. The bowl is sturdy enough to fill with jewel-bright fruits, chocolate eggs, or pretty balls of yarn. The other containers bring a breath of spring to pots and jars, to show off your needles or a bunch of spring flowers.

Pattern on page **100**

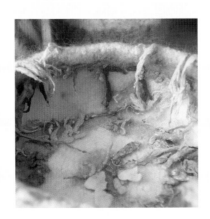

BRAMBLE
STRIPE BAG

Inspired by brambles in autumn when the leaves
turn flame edged and tinged with yellow. Sturdy
and generously sized, this felted bag can be used
for storing projects or for a weekend away if
travelling light.

Pattern on page **104**

BIRCH GILET

Inspired by silver birch trees, this versatile garment makes a great addition to your wardrobe for both work and play. Adding a light yet warming layer, this is a great piece for autumnal walks in the woods or worn with smarter wear for work days.

Pattern on page **106**

SNUG BED SOCKS

This is a luxurious knit, with a neatly tailored toe and no-wrap heel. The socks are embellished with a panel of lace that runs along the front of the sock. This combination of **Kidsilk Haze** and **Fine Lace** yields a really lovely soft, warm fabric with an angora feel. Personally blessed with the coldest feet this side of Lapland, I find these extremely cosy in bed, but they are even better when I am wearing them to pose on an elegant cushion by the fire.

Pattern on page **108**

LICHEN COWL

A generous textured cowl knit in luxurious **Alpaca Colour**.
A simple and satisfying knit inspired by vibrant lichen
covered trees and rocks.

Pattern on page **110**

LICHEN MITTS

Partner to the Lichen Cowl, the mitts have an ample
cuff length to keep you warm while leaving your
fingers and thumbs unrestrained.

Pattern on page 111

DAWN WRAP

Inspired by the heavy dew and brooding mists of early autumn mornings, Dawn is knitted in luxurious hazy **Alpaca Colour** and adorned with beads which yield an elegant drape, providing both comfort and a touch of glamour.

Pattern on page 113

DUSK SCARF

A perfect partner to the Dawn Wrap, Dusk denotes the end
of the day when night begins to creep in. Knitted in sock
weight yarn, this scarf will provide enough warmth for an
autumn day without overheating the wearer.

Pattern on page 115

PATTERNS

This section includes all the directions needed to knit and make up the designs, including any special abbreviations and hints and tips from the designers. General abbreviations and further information on the techniques used are given on pages 118-130.

DRIFT FOLDED SHRUG

FINISHED SIZE

152cm (59¾in) x 13cm (5in) in length
measured from cuff to cuff.
25cm (9¾in) wide across rib section and
39cm (15¼in) wide at the cuff, laid flat
before seaming.

YARN

Rowan Baby Merino Silk DK
50g (1¾oz)/135m (147yds) balls
Dawn 672   6 x 50g

NEEDLES

1 pair 4mm (UK 8/US 6) needles
1 pair 4.5mm (UK 7/US 7) needles

OTHER

756 crystal beads size 6
Safety pins

TENSION

26 sts and 34 rows to 10cm/4in over
slipped stitch rib pattern on 4.5mm
(UK 7/US 7) needles.

SPECIAL ABBREVIATIONS

B3 – place 3 beads; use the same technique
detailed on p 122, but instead of placing 1
bead, place 3 tog.
MF = Make fold: pick up the purl bump st 7
rows down, that is the one beside the next
st on your LH needle, and place this st on
your LH needle; knit it and the next st tog.

SMITH SAYS

"This shrug is knitted flat, and
then seamed. You leave the back
opening at the width that fits you,
and then seam the arms to
the armpits.

The ribbed section will be the
part that goes all the way up your
arm, across your back, and down
the other arm, before you begin
to knit the second folded, beaded
cuff section. Therefore, you can
easily adjust the length slightly
there to suit you."

SHRUG

Thread on beads. Using 4mm needles cast on 86 sts.

Beg with a K row, work 6 rows in st st, ending with RS facing for next row.

Next row (RS): Purl (fold line).

Beg with a purl row, work 7 rows in st st, ending with RS facing for next row.

Folded sleeve section

Rows 1 to 4 (RS): Beg with a K row, work 4 rows in st st.

Row 5 (RS): K2, *B3, k7, rep from * to last 4 sts, B3, k3.

Rows 6 to 9: Beg with a P row, work 4 rows in st st.

Row 10 (WS): P5, *MF 4 times, p4, rep from * to last st, p1.

Rows 11 to 14: Beg with a K row, work 4 rows in st st.

Row 15 (RS): K6, *B3, k7, rep from * to end.

Rows 16 to 19: Beg with a P row, work 4 rows in st st.

Row 20 (WS): P1, *MF 4 times, p4, rep from * to last st, p1.

The last 20 rows form beaded folded patt. Rep these 20 rows twice more, ending with RS facing for next row (60 patt rows worked).

Next row (RS): K6, k2tog, *k10, k2tog, rep from * to last 6 sts, k6. 79 sts.

Next row: Purl.

Next row: K5, k2tog, *k9, k2tog, rep from * to last 6 sts, k6. 72 sts.

Next row: Purl.

Next row: K4, k2tog, *k8, k2tog, rep from * to last 6 sts, k6. 65 sts.

Change to 4.5 mm needles.

Rib section

Row 1 (RS): *K1, with the yarn at the front, slip next st purlwise, take yarn back, rep from * to last st, k1.

Row 2: Purl.

These 2 rows form slipped stitch rib. Cont in rib until the shrug measures approx 136cm (53½in) from the purled fold line at the cuff, ending with RS facing for next row.

Change to 4mm needles.

Next row (RS): K4, kfb, *k8, kfb, rep from * to last 6 sts, k6. 72 sts.

Next row: Purl.

Next row: K5, kfb, *k9, kfb, rep from * to last 6 sts, k6 79 sts.

Next row: Purl.

Next row: K6, kfb, *k10, kfb, rep from * to last 6 sts, k6. 86 sts.

Next row: Purl.

Folded sleeve section

(this is a mirror image of the section you first worked):

Rows 1 to 4: Beg with a K row, work 4 rows in st st.

Row 5 (RS): K6, *B3, k7, rep from * to end.

Rows 6 to 9: Beg with a P row, work 4 rows in st st.

Row 10 (WS): P1, *MF 4 times, p4, rep from * to last st, p1.

Rows 11 to 14: Beg with a K row, work 4 rows in st st.

Row 15 (RS): K2, *B3, k7, rep from * to last 4 sts, B3, k3.

Rows 16 to 19: Beg with a purl row, work 4 rows in st st.

Row 20 (WS): P5, *MF 4 times, p4, rep from * to last st, p1.

The last 20 rows form the beaded folded cuff section. Rep these 20 rows twice more, ending with RS facing for next row (60 patt rows worked).

Beg with a K row, work 6 rows in st st, ending with RS facing for next row.

Next row (RS): Purl (to form fold line).

Beg with a P row, work 6 rows in st st, ending with WS facing for next row.

Cast off.

MAKING UP

Sew in ends. With WS facing, fold the edges of the cuffs down at the purl line and slip stitch into place. With WS facing, pin the shrug out and referring to ball band for specific instructions, and using a damp cloth and a cool iron, carefully block the shrug, taking care not to crush the folds or over-block the rib. Pin the arms of the shrug together and carefully slip it on, so you can determine how much of an un-seamed gap you will need for it to fit you. There should be sufficient gap for you to comfortably get into the shrug whilst ensuring the armhole fits snugly. Mark these points with safety pins. Join side seams using back stitch, or mattress stitch if desired.

ICE BOA IN COCOON

FINISHED SIZE

92.5cm (36½in) in length at cast on edge,
16cm (6¼in) deep.
Note: length will increase naturally
with wear.

YARN

Rowan Cocoon

100g (3½oz) 115m (126yd) balls
Moon 836   3 x 100g

NEEDLES

8mm (UK 0/US 11) fixed cable circular
needle, 100cm (40in) long, or longer
(used flat)

TENSION

12 sts and 16 rows over 10cm (4in) over
st st on 8mm (UK 0/US 11) needles.

SMITH SAYS

"For best results use the thumb
or a long tail cast-on as this
better complements the garter
stitch edging.

The cast off is a picot cast off.
Note that this takes approximately
4 times as much yarn as a
conventional cast off.

The lace or knitted cast on (used
as part of the picot cast off) is
worked as follows: Insert the RH
into the st as if to knit, work a knit
stitch, but do NOT slip it off of the
left needle. Instead transfer the
loop formed back onto the
LH needle."

BOA

Using 7mm needles, cast on 111 sts.

Knit 4 rows.

Row 1 (RS): P7, *k1, p7, rep from * to end.

Row 2: K7, *p1, k7, rep from * to end.

Row 3: P7, *yrn, k1, yfrn, p7, rep from * to end. 137 sts.

Row 4: K7, *p2, p1tbl, k7, rep from * to end.

Row 5: P7, *yrn, k3, yfrn, p7, rep from * to end. 163 sts.

Row 6: K7, *p4, p1tbl, k7, rep from * to end.

Row 7: P7, *yrn, k5, yfrn, p7, rep from * to end. 189 sts.

Row 8: K7, *p6, p1tbl, k7, rep from * to end.

Row 9: P7, *yrn, k7, yfrn, p7, rep from * to end. 215 sts.

Row 10: K7, *p8, p1tbl, k7, rep from * to end.

Row 11: P7, *yrn, k9, yfrn, p7, rep from * to end. 241 sts.

Row 12: K7, *p10, p1tbl, k7, rep from * to end.

Row 13: P7, *yrn, k5, yfrn, p1, yrn, k5, yfrn, p7, rep from * to end. 293 sts.

Row 14: K7, *p6, p1tbl, k1, p6, p1tbl, k7, rep from * to end.

Row 15: P7, *yrn, k6, yfrn, p3, yrn, k6, yfrn, p7, rep from * to end. 345 sts.

Row 16: K7, *p7, p1tbl, k3, p7, p1tbl, k7, rep from * to end.

Row 17: P7, *yrn, k7, yfrn, p5, yrn, k7, yfrn, p7, rep from * to end. 397 sts.

Row 18: K7, *p8, p1tbl, k5, p8, p1tbl, k7, rep from * to end.

Row 19: P7, *yrn, k8, yfrn, p7, yrn, k8, yfrn, p7, rep from * to end. 449 sts.

Row 20: K7, *p9, p1tbl, k7, p9, p1tbl, k7, rep from * to end.

Row 21: P7, *yrn, k9, yfrn, p9, yrn, k9, yfrn, p7, rep from * to end. 501 sts.

Row 22: K7, *p10, p1tbl, k9, p10, p1tbl, k7, rep from * to end.

Picot cast off (RS): *Using the lace (knit) cast on method, cast on 2 sts to the LH needle, cast off 4 sts, slip the rem st on the RH needle onto the LH needle, rep from * to end.

MAKING UP

Sew in ends. No need to block but you could spray lightly with water, pin out the top garter st edge to length and leave to dry.

RIME FAIRISLE SNOOD

FINISHED SIZE

50.5cm (19¾in) wide laid flat, or 101cm (39¾in) circumference and 98cm (38½in) long.

YARN

Rowan Kidsilk Haze

25g (1oz)/210m (230yds) balls

A Wicked 599	3 x 25g
B Smoke 605	2 x 25g
C Steel 664	3 x 25g
D White 612	3 x 25g

NEEDLES

4.5mm (UK 7/US 7) fixed cable circular needle, 80 or 100cm (32 or 40in) long
5mm (UK 6/US 8) fixed cable circular needle, 80 or 100cm (32 or 40in) long

OTHER

Approx 700 crystal beads, size 6
1 stitch marker

TENSION

19 sts and 20 rnds to 10cm/4ins over fairisle pattern worked in the round using Kidsilk Haze held DOUBLE on 5mm (UK 6/US 8) needles.

SPECIAL ABBREVIATIONS

PB = place a bead on the next stitch (see notes on p 122)

SMITH SAYS

"The colourwash is simple, and this all takes place in the background yarns. The accent yarn – white – never changes. This yarn both creates the simple Fairisle pattern, and carries the beads.

Yarns used double throughout; expressed as AA, BB, CC, DD, AB, BC etc.

Yarn D (white) is the accent colour and is always knitted as 2 strands of D together; this yarn is also the yarn that carries the beads. It is expressed as yarn DD and is only blended with another shade (C) in the last pattern repeat and the finishing rib section.

Thread the beads on (see notes 118) in batches of 200 – 250 at a time. When you need more, break yarns and thread on more beads. This saves wear on the yarn."

SNOOD

Thread beads onto yarn DD, held double.

Using yarn AA and 4.5mm needle cast on 192 sts. Taking care not to twist cast on edge, join to knit in the round, place marker.

Border

Rnd 1: *K1 tbl, p1, rep from * to end.

Rnd 1 forms 1 x 1 twisted rib. Work in rib for 6cm (2¼ in).

Next rnd (fold line): Purl.

Cont in rib for 6cm (2¼ in).

Fairisle Pattern

Change to 5mm needle.

Rnds 1 to 4: Knit using yarn AA.

Rnds 5 to 15: Using yarn AA as background and yarn DD for fairisle and beaded motif, work 11 rounds as set on chart A.

Rnds 16 to 19: Knit using yarn AA, knit, carrying yarn DD up work as you go.

Rnds 20 to 24: Work 5 rnds as set on chart B.

Rnds 25 to 28: Knit using yarn AA, knit, carrying yarn DD up work as you go. 28 rnds of Main Pattern worked.

Rnds 29 to 56: Work rnds 1 to 28, using yarn AB as background.

Rnds 57 to 84: Work rnds 1 to 28, using yarn BB as background.

Rnds 85 to 112: Work rnds 1 to 28, using yarn BC as background.

Rnds 113 to 140: Work rnds 1 to 28, using yarn CC as background.

Rnds 141 to 168: Work rnds 1 to 28, using yarn CD as background.

Knit 4 rnds using yarn CD.

Border

Change to 4.5mm needle.

Work 6cm (2¼ in) in twisted rib as at beg, using yarn CD.

Next rnd (fold line): Purl.

Work 6cm (2¼ in) in twisted rib.

Cast off in rib.

MAKING UP

Turn the piece inside out. Taking care not to affect tension, at the cast on edge fold the work at the purl line and with yarn AA, slip stitch the cast on border edge down. At the cast off end, sew the border edge down with yarn C & D held together.

Refer to ball band for specific instructions. Pin the work (which will be folded in half because it is knitted in the round) to a thick sheet or bath towels. Cover with a damp fine cloth. With a steam iron on a cool setting, and hovering and skimming, not pressing down, gently block the piece. Remove the cloth. Unpin the work and turn it over. Remove the cloth(s). Leave to dry before unpinning.

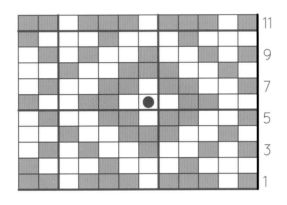

Yarn

☐ Main Colour
▨ Background Colour

Stitches

☐ K
◉ PB

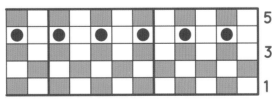

Yarn

☐ Main Colour
▨ Background Colour

Stitches

☐ K
◉ PB

ICE BOA

SIZE

107cm (42¼in) in length at cast on edge
(which is the shortest point), and 17cm
(6¾in) deep.
Note: length will increase naturally
with wear.

YARN

Rowan Kidsilk Haze
25g (1oz)/210m (230 yds) balls
A Cream 634   4 x 25g
Rowan Fine Lace
50g (1¾oz)/400m (237yd) balls
B Porcelaine 928   2 x 50g

NEEDLES

5mm (UK 6/US 8) fixed cable circular
needle, at least 100cm (40in) long (used
flat)
6mm (UK 4/US 10) needle for the cast off
rows only

OTHER

624 crystal beads, size 6

TENSION

20 sts and 22 rows to 10cm/4in over st st
with A & B held together on 5mm needles.

SPECIAL ABBREVIATIONS

PB = place a bead on the next stitch. In
this pattern, unlike the cuffs, the beads are
placed with the wrong side facing
(see p123).

SMITH SAYS

"Yarns A & B are held
together throughout.

For best results use the thumb
or a long tail cast-on as this
better complements the garter
stitch edging.

I threaded beads on in batches of
about 200.

The cast off is a scalloped lace
cast off; note that this cast off
takes 5 times as much yarn as a
conventional cast off.

As this boa is very long, you may
wish to shorten it; if so the pattern
is a multiple of 8 stitches plus 7."

BOA

Thread beads onto yarn A & B, held together.

Using 5mm needle cast on 215 sts.
Work 8 rows in garter st.

Main boa

Row 1 (RS): P7, *k1, p7, rep from * to end.

Row 2: K7, *p1, k7, rep from * to end.

Row 3: P7, * yrn, k1, yfrn, p7, rep from * to end. 267 sts.

Row 4: K7, *p1, PB, p1tbl, k7, rep from * to end.

Row 5: P7, *yrn, k3, yfrn, p7, rep from * to end. 319 sts.

Row 6: K7, *p1, PB, p1, PB, p1tbl, k7, rep from * to end.

Row 7: P7, *yrn, k5, yfrn, p7, rep from * to end. 371 sts.

Row 8: K7, *p1, PB, p3, PB, p1tbl, k7, rep from * to end.

Cont as set, placing increases on odd numbered rows and placing beads on even numbered rows until you have reached Row 12 which will be worked thus:

Row 12 (WS): K7, *p1, PB, p7, PB, p1tbl, k7, rep from * to end. 475 sts.

Now we will add in the extra frill:

Row 13: P7, *yrn, k5, yfrn, p1, yrn, k5, yfrn, p7, rep from * to end. 579 sts.

Row 14: K7, *p1, PB, p4, p1tbl, k1, p5, PB, p1tbl, k7, rep from * to end.

Row 15: P7, *yrn, k6, yfrn, p3, yrn, k6, yfrn, p7, rep from * to end. 683 sts.

Row 16: K7, *p1, PB, p5, p1tbl, k3, p6, PB, p1tbl, k7, rep from * to end.

Row 17: P7, *yrn, k7, yfrn, p5, yrn, k7, yfrn, p7, rep from * to end. 787 sts.

Row 18: K7, *p1, PB, p6, p1tbl, k5, p7, PB, p1tbl, k7, rep from * to end.

Row 19: P7, *yrn, k8, yfrn, p7, yrn, k8, yfrn, p7, rep from * to end. 891 sts.

Row 20: K7, *p1, PB, p7, p1tbl, k7, p8, PB, p1tbl, k7, rep from * to end.

Row 21: P7, *yrn, k9, yfrn, p9, yrn, k9, yfrn, p7, rep from * to end. 995 sts.

Row 22: K7, *p1, PB, p8, p1tbl, k9, p9, PB, p1tbl, k7, rep from * to end.

Cont as set, placing beads on even numbered rows and increasing on odd numbered rows for 6 more rows. 1619 sts. Change to 6mm needles.

Cast off: K1, *(sl this st back to the LH needle, knit into the st and knit it off) 3 times, k1, cast off 1 st, rep from * to end. (This forms a 3 st 'chain' between cast off sts).

Top frill

With RS facing, using 5mm needles pick up and knit 215 sts along the cast on edge of the boa. NB: This number is not absolutely critical, so if you are few out, don't worry about it.

Knit 1 row.

Row 1 (RS): *Kfb, rep from * to end. 430 sts.

Row 2: Knit.

Row 3: As row 2. 860 sts.

With WS facing, using a 6mm needle, cast off knit-wise and purl-wise alternately, keeping the tension relaxed.

MAKING UP

Sew in ends. No need to block and press but you could pin out and lightly spray the garter st section with water, and allow to dry fully before unpinning.

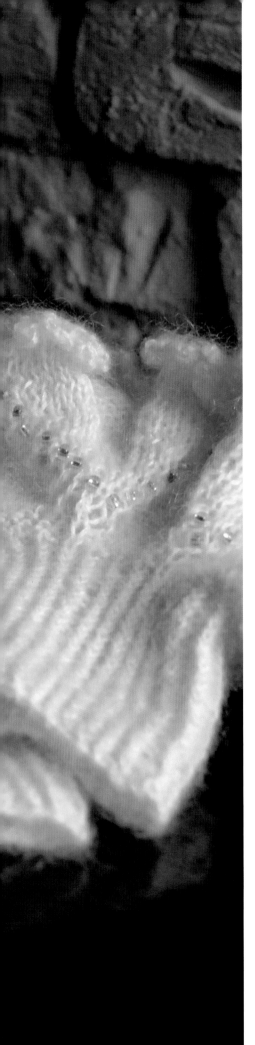

ICE CUFFS

SIZE

To fit snugly around average female wrist,
17cm (6¾in) in length from cast on to cast
off edges when laid out flat, unstretched.

YARN

Rowan Kidsilk Haze

25g (1oz)/210m (230 yds) balls

A Cream 634   2 x 25g

Rowan Fine Lace

50g (1¾oz)/400m (237yd) balls

B Porcelaine 928   1 x 50g

NEEDLES

Set of 2.75mm (UK 12/US 2) DPNs
Set of 4mm (UK 8/US 6) DPNs, 20cm/8in
long
1 pair 5mm (UK 6/US 8) needles for the
cast off.

OTHER

Stitch marker
294 crystal beads, size 6

TENSION

40 sts and 42 rnds to 10cm/4in over twisted
rib, worked in the round with A&B held
together on 2.75mm (UK 12/US 2) needles.

SPECIAL ABBREVIATIONS

PB = place a bead on the next stitch. In this
pattern, unlike the Ice Boa, the beads are
placed with the right side facing (see p 122)

SMITH SAYS

"Yarns A & B are held
together throughout.

For best results use the thumb or
a long tail cast-on as this better
complements the rib edging.

The cast off is a scalloped lace
cast off; note that this cast off
takes 5 times as much yarn as a
conventional cast off."

CUFF (make 2 alike)

Thread beads onto yarns A & B held tog.

Using 2.75mm (US 2) needles cast on 56 sts.
Taking care not to twist cast on edge,
arrange on 3 DPNs. Place beg of round
marker and join to knit in the round.

Ribbed section

Rnd 1: *K1 tbl, p1, rep from * to end.

Rnd 1 sets twisted rib patt. Cont in rib until
work measures 7cm (2¾in).

Main cuff

Change to 4mm (US 6) needles.

Rnd 1: *K1, p7, rep from * to end.

Rnd 2: As rnd 1.

Rnd 3: *Yrn, k1, yfrn, p7, rep from * to end.
70 sts.

Rnd 4: *K1 tbl, PB, k1, p7, rep from * to end.

Rnd 5: *Yrn, k3, yfrn, p7, rep from * to end.
84 sts.

Rnd 6: *K1 tbl, PB, k1, PB, k1, p7, rep from
* to end.

Rnd 7: *Yrn, k5, yfrn, p7, rep from * to end.
98 sts.

Rnd 8: *K1 tbl, PB, k3, PB, k1, p7, rep from
* to end.

Rnd 9: *Yrn, k7, yfrn, p7, rep from * to end.
112 sts.

Rnd 10: *K1 tbl, PB, k5, PB, k1, p7, rep from
* to end.

Rnd 11: *Yrn, k9, yfrn, p7, rep from * to end.
126 sts.

Rnd 12: *K1 tbl, PB, k7, PB, k1, p7, rep from
* to end.

Rnd 13: *Yrn, k5, yfrn, p1, yrn, k5, yfrn, p7,
rep from * to end. 154 sts.

Rnd 14: *K1 tbl, PB, k4, p2, p1 tbl, k4, PB, k1,
p7, rep from * to end.

Rnd 15: *Yrn, k6, yfrn, p3, yrn, k6, yfrn, p7,
rep from * to end. 182 sts.

Rnd 16: *K1 tbl, PB, k5, p4, p1 tbl, k5, PB, k1,
p7, rep from * to end.

Rnd 17: *Yrn, k7, yfrn, p5, yrn, k7, yfrn, p7,
rep from * to end. 210 sts.

Rnd 18: *K1 tbl, PB, k6, p6, p1 tbl, k6, PB, k1,
p7, rep from * to end.

Rnd 19: *Yrn, k8, yfrn, p7, yrn, k8, yfrn, p7,
rep from * to end. 238 sts.

Rnd 20: *K1 tbl, PB, k7, p8, p1 tbl, k7, PB, k1,
p7, rep from * to end.

Rnd 21: *Yrn, k9, yfrn, p9, yrn, k9, yfrn, p7,
rep from * to end. 266 sts.

Rnd 22: *K1 tbl, PB, k8, p10, p1 tbl, k8, PB,
k1, p7, rep from * to end.

Rnd 23: *Yrn, k10, yfrn, p11, yrn, k10, yfrn,
p7, rep from * to end. 294 sts.

Rnd 24: *K1 tbl, PB, k9, p12, p1 tbl, k9, PB,
k1, p7, rep from * to end.

Rnd 25: *Yrn, k11, yfrn, p13, yrn, k11, yfrn,
p7, rep from * to end. 322 sts.

Change to 5mm needles.

Cast off: K1, *(sl this st back to the LH
needle, knit into the st and knit it off) 3
times, k1, cast off 1 st, rep from * to end.
(This forms a 3 st 'chain' between cast off
sts).

MAKING UP

Sew in ends. No need to block or press.

DRIFT FOLDED CUFF MITTS

SIZE

To fit average female hand approximately 20cm (8in) circumference above thumb. Mitts measure 18cm (7¼in) from fold-line at cuff to fold-line at fingers.

YARN

Rowan Baby Merino Silk DK
50g (1¾oz)/135m (147yds) balls
Dawn 672   2 x 50g

NEEDLES

Set of 3mm (UK 11/US 2-3) DPNs or size required to achieve correct tension

OTHER

3 stitch markers
168 crystal beads, size 6
Safety pin or length of waste yarn for thumb stitches

TENSION

26 sts and 32 rounds to 10cm/4in in moss stitch rib worked in the round on 3mm (UK11/US 2-3) double pointed needles.

SPECIAL ABBREVIATIONS

MF = Make fold: reaching down into the inside of the mitten, pick up the purl bump st 7 rnds down, that is the one beside the next st on your LH needle, and place this st on your LH needle; knit this and the next st tog.
PB = place a bead on the next stitch (see notes on p 122).
TM1 = thumb marker 1.
TM2 = thumb marker 2.
STM1/2 = slip thumb marker 1/2.

SMITH SAYS

"It is helpful to have 3 stitch markers which are different from each other – 1 colour each for the main marker and 2 thumb markers."

MITTS (make 2 alike)

Cast on 56 sts.

Taking care not to twist cast on edge, arrange on 3 DPNs. Place beg of round marker and join to knit in the round.

Rnds 1 to 4: Knit.

Rnd 5 (fold line): Purl.

Rnds 6 to 9: Knit.

Folded Beaded Section

Rnds 1 to 4: Knit.

Rnd 5: *K3, PB, rep from * to end.

Rnds 6 to 9: Knit

Rnd 10: *K4, MF 4 times, rep from * to end.

Rnds 11 to 14: Knit.

Rnd 15: K1, * PB, k3, rep from * to last 3 sts, PB, k2.

Rnds 16 to 19: Knit.

Rnd 20: *MF 4 times, k4, rep from * to end.

These 20 rnds form beaded folded cuff patt. Rep these 20 rnds once more (40 rnds of patt worked).

Next rnd: K3, k2tog, rep from * to last st, k1. 45 sts.

Next rnd: K2, k2tog, *k6, k2tog, rep from * to last 9 sts, k9. 40 sts.

Moss stitch rib section

Rnd 1: *K3, p1, rep from * to end.

Rnd 2: *P1, k1, p2, rep from * to end.

Last 2 rnds form moss st rib patt. Work in patt for a further 6 rnds.

Thumb gusset

Rnd 1: Work 8 sts, k1, place TM1, yfwd, k1, yfwd, place TM2, k1, patt to end.

Rnd 2: Work 8 sts, k1, STM1, k3, STM2, k1, patt to end.

Rnd 3: Work 8 sts, k1, STM1, yfwd, k3, yfwd, STM2, k1, patt to end.

Rnd 4: Work 8 sts, k1, STM1, k5, STM2, k1, patt to end.

Cont as set until you have worked this rnd: Work 8 sts, k1, STM1, yfwd, k15, yfwd, STM2, k1, patt to end.

Next rnd: Work 8 sts, k1, STM1, k17, STM2, k1, patt to end.

Next rnd: Work 8 sts, k1, remove TM1, slip next 17 sts onto safety pin, remove TM2, cast on 3 sts to RH needle, reach across the

gap, k1, patt to end. 42 sts.

Next rnd: Work 8 sts, k2tog, k1, k2tog, patt to end. 40 sts.

Work 2 rnds in moss st rib patt.

Next rnd: K3, *kfb, k6, rep from * to last 2 sts, k2. 45 sts.

Next rnd: *K3, kfb, rep from * to last st, k1. 56 sts.

Work rnds 1-20 of Folded beaded section as set.

Rnds 21 to 23: Knit.

Rnd 24 (fold line): Purl.

Rnds 25 to 27: Knit.

Cast off loosely.

Thumb

Slip the 17 thumb sts onto 2 DPNs. With RS facing and 3rd DPN, pick up and knit 5 sts where you cast on 3 sts earlier. 22 sts. Place main st marker and join to work in the round.

Next Rnd: K to last 5 sts, k2tog, k1, k2tog. 20 sts.

Knit 3 rnds.

Cont in moss st rib patt for a further 6 rnds or as desired to fit length of thumb.

Cast off in patt.

MAKING UP

Sew in ends. Fold the cuff and finger edges down at the fold-line and, taking care not to affect the tension/elasticity in the fit of the mitten, slip-stitch down on the WS. No need to press.

RISE SCARF

FINISHED SIZE

16cm (6¼in) wide laid flat (or 32cm/12½in circumference) and 141cm (55½in) long

YARN

Rowan Pure Wool 4 Ply
50g (1¾oz)/160m (174yds) balls
A Eau de Nil   4 x 50g
Anchor Artiste Metallic
25g (1oz)100m (109yds) balls
B Silver 301   6 x 25g

NEEDLES

1 pair 3mm (UK11/US 2- 3) needles
1 pair 3.25mm (UK 10/US 3) needles

TENSION

32 sts and 56 rows to 10cm/4in measured over pattern on 3.25mm (US 2 – 3) needles.

SPECIAL ABBREVIATIONS

Sl 2 wyaf = with the yarn at the front of your work, slip the next 2 sts from the LH to the RH needle, without working them.
Sl 2 wyab = with the yarn at the back of your work, slip the next 2 sts from the LH to the RH needle, without working them.

SMITH SAYS

"Although this scarf is circular, it is knitted in two pieces and then seamed together.

Yarn A becomes Yarn B and vice versa for the second side of the scarf.

Carry yarn not in use up the sides of the work, taking care not to pull too tight as you twist the yarns.

For the purpose of matching the 'cells' at the side seams, it is important to knit exactly the same number of pattern repeats for each side.

Any yarns of contrasting colour or even, within reason, ply, could be used if you adjust the needle size."

SCARF

Side 1

Using 3mm (US 2 – 3) needles and A, cast on 54 sts.

Knit 5 rows. **

Main patt

Change to 3.25mm (US 3) needles.

Rows 1 and 2: Knit.

Change to yarn B.

Row 3 (RS): K2, *sl 2 wyab, k6, rep from * to last 4 sts, sl 2 wyab, k2.

Row 4: P2, *sl 2 wyaf, p6, rep from * to last 4 sts, sl 2 wyaf, p2.

Rows 5: As row 3

Row 6: As row 4.

Row 7: As row 3.

Row 8: As row 4.

Change to yarn A.

Rows 9 to 12: Knit.

Change to yarn B.

Row 13: *K6, sl 2 wyab, rep from * to last 6 sts, k6.

Row 14: P6, *sl 2 wyaf, p6, rep from * to end.

Row 15: As row 13.

Row 16: As row 14.

Row 17: As row 13.

Row 18: As row 14.

Change to yarn A.

Rows 19 and 20: Knit.

Rep last 20 rows until work measures 140cm (55in), ending with Row 20 and RS facing for next row.

Change to 3mm (US 2 – 3) needles.

Knit 5 rows.

Cast off knitwise.

Side 2

Work as for Side 1 to **.

Then, work as for Side 1, reversing the colourways, but working the final 5 knit rows in yarn A.

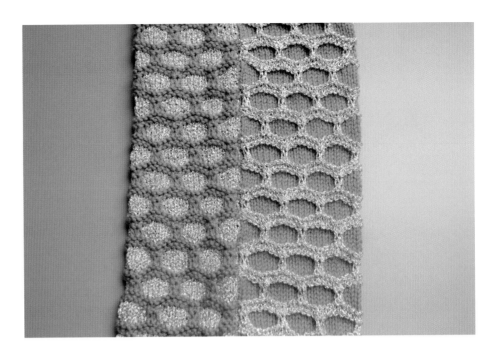

MAKING UP

Sew in ends. Using ball bands as a guide, and with WS facing, gently block and press both sides.

With RS tog, carefully seam the scarf edges together, taking care to 'match' the cells (see photograph as a guide).

LANDSCAPE THROW

FINISHED SIZE

80cm (31½in) X 206cm (81in)

YARN

Rowan Cocoon

100g (3½oz) 115m (126yd) balls

A Crag 809	3 x 100g
B Seascape 813	3 x 100g
C Duckdown 833	3 x 100g
D Polar 801	6 x 100g

NEEDLES

7mm (UK 2/US 10 ½ - 11) fixed cable
circular needle, 100cm (40in) or longer
in length

OTHER

Cable needle

TENSION

14 sts and 18 rows in Broken Rib pattern
over 10cm/4in square, using 7mm needles.

SPECIAL ABBREVIATIONS

C8B = place the next 4 sts on the cable
needle and hold at the back of the work,
knit the next 4 sts on the left hand needle,
knit the 4 sts on the cable needle.

C8F = place the next 4 sts on the cable
needle and hold at the front of the work,
knit the next 4 sts on the left hand needle,
knit the 4 sts on the cable needle.

SMITH SAYS

"The design is worked in rows
using the intarsia colour-work
technique (see page 125).

Leave approximately 20cm (8in)
long ends when you need to start
a new ball of each colour as this
will aid neat and secure weaving
in. Avoid joining in right at the
edges, but instead try and join in
at, or just after, the 7 stitch edges.

The 'background' to the throw is
worked in a textured broken rib
stitch, in deep blocks of colour.
The cable panels are worked in
between these sections. The cable
panels are all worked only in yarn
D; the panels of pattern are both
12 rows long. Thus you will work
Row 1 of Broken Rib, Row 1 of Cable
Panel, and repeat across the row;
the row numbers worked from
each panel, as you work across the
row, will always be the same.

The first time you work the Cable
Pattern panel repeat, the pattern
varies slightly – see Cable Panel
Patterns below."

PANEL A

Broken Rib Pattern

(each panel is 18 sts wide):

Row 1 (RS): (K4, p2) 3 times.

Row 2: (K2, p4) 3 times.

Row 3: As row 1.

Row 4: As row 2.

Row 5: K2, (p2, k4) twice, p2, k2.

Row 6: P2, (k2, p4) twice, k2, p2.

Row 7: As row 5.

Row 8: As row 6.

Row 9: (P2, k4) 3 times.

Row 10: As row 2.

Row 11: As row 9.

Row 12: As row 2.

These 12 rows form Broken Rib Pattern.

PANEL B

Cable Pattern **for the first repeat only**

(each panel is 26 sts wide)

Row 1 (RS): K26.

Row 2 & all WS rows: K5, p16, k5.

Row 3: P3, k20, P3.

Row 5: P3, k2, C8B twice, k2, p3.

Row 7: As Row 3.

Row 9: As Row 3.

Row 11: P3, k6, C8F, k6, p3.

Row 12: As Row 2.

CABLE PATTERN FOR ALL FOLLOWING REPEATS

Row 1 (RS): P3, k20, p3.

Row 2 & all RS rows: K5, p16, k5.

Row 3: As row 1.

Row 5: P3, k2, C8B twice, k2, p3.

Row 7: As Row 1.

Row 9: As Row 1.

Row 11: P3, k6, C8F, k6, p3.

Row 12: As Row 2.

These 12 rows set Cable Pattern.

THROW

Using 7mm (US 10½-11) needles and yarn A, cast on 104 sts.

Knit 7 rows.

Next row (inc): K28, *(k1, inc once in each of next 3 sts, k1) twice, k28, rep from * to end. 116 sts.

Foundation row (WS): With yarn A, K5, * with yarn A (K2, p4) 3 times, change to yarn D, k26, rep from * to last 23 sts, with yarn A (K2, p4) 3 times, k5.

Main pattern

Note: For the first repeat only, you will work the first set of instructions for panel B above

Row 1 (RS): With yarn A, K5, *with yarn A work row 1 of Panel A, change to yarn D and work row 1 of Panel B, rep from * to last 23 sts, with yarn A work row 1 of Panel A, k5.

Row 2: With yarn A K5, * with yarn A work row 2 of Panel A, change to yarn D and work row 2 of Panel B, rep from * to last 23 sts, with yarn A work row 2 of Panel A, k5.

Row 3: With yarn A, K5, * work row 3 of Panel A, change to yarn D and work row 3 of Panel B, rep from * to last 23 sts, with yarn A work row 3 of Panel A, k5.

Row 4: With yarn A, K5, *with yarn A work row 4 of Panel A, change to yarn D, work row 4 of Panel B, rep from * to last 23 sts, with yarn A work row 4 of Panel A, k5.

Cont as set, working appropriate rows from each panel patt and always knitting the first and last 5 sts on every row, work a further 24 rows.

Cont as set, using Yarn D throughout for both Panel B sections and substituting colours for border and Panel A sections as follows.

Rows 37 to 72: Yarn B for the edges and Panel A sections.

Rows 73 to 108: Yarn C for the edges and Panel A sections.

Rep these 108 rows twice more, and rows 1-36 once, ending with RS facing for next row.

Next row (RS) (dec): K28, *(k1, k2tog 3 times, k1) twice, k28, rep from * to end. 104 sts.

With yarn A, knit 6 rows, ending with WS facing for next row.

Cast off knitwise ensuring that your tension is relaxed and matches that of the cast-on edge.

MAKING UP

Sew in ends. Finish by pinning out to shape with WS facing, spray lightly with water and leave to dry; or with a damp cloth and a steam iron set to cool, hover the iron over the work (do not press down).

LANDSCAPE CUSHION

FINISHED SIZE
56cm (22in) x 56cm (22in)

YARN
Rowan Cocoon
100g (3½ oz) 115m (126yd) balls
A Crag 809   2 x 100g
B Seascape 813   1 x 100g
C Duckdown 833   1 x 100g
D Polar 801   4 x 100g

NEEDLES
7mm (UK 2/US 10½ - 11) needles

OTHER
Cable needle
3 X 3.5cm (1¾in) buttons (see Resources
p 131)
Cushion pad 56cm (22in) x 56cm (22in)

TENSION
14 sts and 18 rows to 10cm/4in over
Broken Rib pattern on 7mm (UK 2/US
10½) needles.
19 sts and 21 rows to 10cm/4in over Cable
pattern on 7mm (UK 2/US 10½) needles.

SPECIAL ABBREVIATIONS
C8F = place the next 4 sts on the cable
needle and hold at the front of the work,
knit the next 4 sts on the left hand needle,
knit the 4 sts on the cable needle.
C8B = place the next 4 sts on the cable
needle and hold at the back of the work,
knit the next 4 sts on the left hand needle,
knit the 4 sts on the cable needle.
MBH = make button hole (made
horizontally over 1 row): (Yfwd, sl1
purlwise, yb, sl1 purlwise, with LH needle,
pass the first slipped st over the st just
slipped) 6 times, turn; using cable cast-on,
cast on 7 sts, yfwd, turn; with yarn at the
back and RS facing, sl the next st from the
LH needle to the RH needle, pass the extra
st on the RH needle over the slipped st.

FRONT

Using 7mm (US 10½) needles and D, cast on 106 sts.

Cable Pattern

Row 1 (RS): Knit.

Row 2 (and all WS rows): K1, p to last st, k1.

Row 3: Knit.

Row 5: K1, *C8B, rep from * to last st, k1.

Row 7: Knit

Row 9: Knit.

Row 11: K5, *C8F, rep from * to last 5 sts, k5.

Row 12: As row 2.

These 12 rows set out Cable Pattern.

Cont in patt until work measures 56cm (22in), ending with RS facing for next row.

Cast off loosely.

UPPER BACK

Using 7mm (US 10½) needles and A, cast on 78 sts.

Broken Rib Pattern

Row 1 (RS): *K4, p2, rep from * to end.

Row 2: *K2, p4, rep from * to end.

Row 3: As row 1.

Row 4: As row 2.

Row 5: K2, *p2, k4, rep from * to last 4 sts, p2, k2.

Row 6: P2, *k2, p4, rep from * to last 4 sts, k2, p2.

Row 7: As row 5.

Row 8: As row 6.

Row 9: *P2, k4, rep from * to end.

Row 10: *K2, p4, rep from * to end.

Row 11: As Row 9.

Row 12: As Row 10.

These 12 rows set Broken Rib Pattern.

Work rows 1 – 3 once more, ending with WS facing for next row.

Button hole row (WS): (K2, p4) twice, k2, p1, MBH, p3, (k2, p4) twice, MBH, (k2, p4) twice, k2, p1, MBH, p3, (k2, p4) twice.

Cont in patt until work measures 18cm (7in), ending RS facing for next row.

Change to Yarn C.

Cont in patt for until work measures 37cm (14½in), ending with RS facing for next row.

Cast off in patt.

LOWER BACK

Using 7mm (US 10½) needles and yarn B, cast on 78 sts.

Working in Broken Rib Pattern as for upper back until work measures 19cm (7½in), ending with RS facing for next row.

Change to yarn A.

Cont in patt until work measures 37cm (14½in), ending with RS facing for next row.

Cast off in patt.

MAKING UP

Sew in ends. With WS facing, pin out pieces and with a damp cloth and iron set to cool, skim the work taking care not to press down. Allow to dry. With right sides together, sew cushion Front and Upper Back together, then sew Lower Back into place so that Yarn A stripe overlaps yarn A stripe of Upper back. Turn RS out and poke the corners out so they are nice and pointy. Sew buttons to correspond with the button holes. Insert cushion pad.

KITCHEN GARDEN TUNIC

FINISHED SIZE

	S	M	L	XL	XXL	
To fit Bust	81-86	91-97	102-107	112-117	122-127	cm
	32-34	36-38	40-42	44-46	48-50	in

YARN

Rowan Wool Cotton 50g (1¾ oz)/ 113m (124yds) balls

A Sage 986	11	12	14	15	16	50g
B Bilberry 969	1	1	1	1	2	50g
C Smalt 963	1	1	1	1	1	50g

NEEDLES

1 pair 4mm (UK 8/US 6) needles
1 pair 3.25mm (UK 10/US 3) needles
4mm (UK 8/US 6) or smaller DPNs x 2

OTHER

4 stitch markers

TENSION

22 sts and 30 rows to 10cm/4in over st st
on 4mm (UK 8/US 6) needles.

SPECIAL ABBREVIATIONS

PM = place marker.
wyab = with yarn at back.
wyaf = with yarn at front

JONES SAYS

" See page 128 for our tutorial on
how to knit the box pleat in place.

Alternatively the pleat can be 'cast
off', folded and stitched in place on
the reverse thus: K 51 [57: 63: 67:
74], cast off next 28 sts, k to end.

For best results use the thumb or
a long tail cast-on as this better
complements the garter
stitch edging."

BACK

Using 3.25mm (US 3) needles and B cast on
134 [146:158:170:180] sts.

Knit 4 rows, ending with RS facing for next
row.

Change to C and knit 4 more rows, ending
with RS facing for next row.

Change to A and 4mm (US 6) needles.

Beg with a k row work 16 rows in stocking
st, ending with RS facing for next row.

Shape sides

Dec 1 st at each end of next and 8 [7: 5: 9:
2] foll 8th rows, then on 7 [8: 10: 7: 13] foll
10th rows. 102 [114: 126: 136: 148] sts.

Next row (WS): Purl.

Change to 3.25mm (US 3) needles and knit
6 rows, ending with RS facing for next row.

Change to 4mm (US 6) needles.

Beg with a k row cont straight in st st until
back measures 65 [66: 67: 68: 69] cm (25½
[26: 26½: 26¾: 27½] in), ending with RS
facing for next row.

Shape armholes

Cast off 5 [6: 7: 8: 9] sts at beg of next 2
rows. 92 [102: 112: 120: 130] sts.

Dec 1 st at each end of next 3 [5: 7: 9: 11]
rows, then on 5 [6: 7: 7: 8] foll alt rows.
76 [80: 84: 88: 92] sts.

Cont straight until armhole measures 20
[21: 22: 23: 24] cm (7¾ [8¼: 8¾: 9: 9½] in),
ending with a RS facing for next row.

Shape back neck and shoulders

Next row (RS): K18 [19: 19: 20: 22] and
turn, leaving remaining sts on a holder.
Work each side of neck separately.

Cast off 3 sts at beg of next row, 6 [6: 6: 7:
8] sts at beg of foll row, then 3 sts at beg of
next row.

Cast off rem 6 [7: 7: 7: 8] sts.

With RS facing, rejoin yarn to rem sts, cast
off centre 40 [42: 46: 48: 48] sts, k to end.
Complete to match first side, reversing
shapings.

FRONT

Using 3.25mm (US 3) needles and B cast
on 186 [198: 210: 222: 232] sts.

Work first row, placing markers at pleat
as follows:

Row 1: K66 [72: 78: 84: 89], PM, sl 1 wyab,
k12, PM, sl 1 wyaf, k26, PM, sl 1 wyaf, k12,
PM, sl 1 wyab, k to end.

Note: Hereafter slip all markers as you
come to them, no further mention will be
made of this.

Row 2: Knit.

Rep these 2 rows once more.

Change to C and rep these 2 rows twice.

Change to A and 4mm (US 6) needles.

Row 9: As row 1.

Row 10: Purl.

Last 2 rows set pattern. Work in patt for 14
rows, ending with RS facing for next row.

Shape sides

Dec 1 st at each end of next and 8 [7: 5: 9:
2] foll 8th rows, then on 7 [8: 10: 7: 13] foll
10th rows, AT SAME TIME dec at central
pleat on foll 7th [7th: 9th: 9th: 11th] row,
then on 5 following 22nd rows thus:

Pleat dec rows (RS): K to st marker, sl 1
wyab, k to within 2 sts of next st marker,
k2tog, sl 1 wyaf, k2tog tbl, k to within 2 sts of
next st marker, k2tog, sl 1 wyaf, k2tog tbl, k
to next st marker, sl1 wyab, k to end.
You will now have worked a total of
159[161: 165: 167: 171] rows, and have a
total of 130 [142: 154: 164: 176] sts.

Next row: Purl, removing stitch markers as
you come to them.

Change to 3.25mm (US 3) needles.

Fold pleat (RS): K44 [50: 56: 61: 67], slip
next 7 sts onto DPN's, slip following 7 sts
onto a second DPN's, fold these in to lie at
front and parallel with sts on LH needle (as
demonstrated in tutorial on p 128). K tog
1 st from each of the 3 pleat layers 7 times
(until the 7 sts have been worked from
the DPN's), slip next 7 sts onto DPN's, slip
following 7 sts onto a second DPN's, fold
these in to lie at back and parallel with sts
on LH needle, k tog 1 st from each of the
3 pleat 7 times (until the 7 sts have been
worked from the DPN's), k to end. 102
[114: 126: 136: 148] sts.

Knit 5 rows, ending with RS facing for next
row.

Change to 4mm needles.

Cont without shaping until front matches
back to armhole shaping, ending with RS
facing for next row.

Shape armholes

Cast off 5 [6: 7: 8: 9] sts at beg of next 2
rows. 92 [102: 112: 120: 130] sts.

Dec 1 st at each end of next 3 [5: 7: 9: 11]
rows, then on 3 [4: 3: 3: 2] foll alt rows.
80 [84: 92: 96: 104] sts.

Next Row (WS): Purl.

Shape front neck and shoulders

Work each side of neck separately, thus:

Next Row (RS): Dec 1 st at armhole edge
and k until there are 30 [32: 35: 37: 41] sts
on RH needle, turn, leaving rem sts on a
holder.

Next Row (WS): Purl.

Cont to dec 1 st at armhole edge on next
and foll 0 [0: 2: 2: 4] alt rows AT SAME TIME
dec at neck edge as follows:

Dec 1 st at neck edge of next 7 rows, then
on 5 [6: 7: 8: 7] foll alt rows, then on 5 [5: 5:
5: 6] foll 4th rows. 12 [13: 13: 14: 16] sts.
Cont without shaping until armhole matches
back to start of shoulder shaping, ending
with RS facing for next row.

Cast off 6 [6: 6: 7: 8] sts, k to end.

Work 1 row.

Cast off rem 6 [7: 7: 7: 8] sts.

With RS facing, rejoin yarn to rem sts, cast
off centre 18 [18: 20: 20: 20] sts, k to end.
Complete to match first side,
reversing shapings.

MAKE POCKET

Using 4mm (US 6) needles and A cast on
35 sts.

Knit 2 rows.

Next row (RS): Knit.

Next row (WS): K2, p to last 2 sts, k2.

Last 2 rows set st st panel with garter stitch
borders.

Cont until work measures 18cm (7in),
ending with RS facing for next row.

Change to C and knit 4 rows, ending with
RS facing for next row.

Change to B and knit 5 rows, ending with
WS facing for next row.

Cast off knitwise.

MAKING UP

Sew in ends on wrong side. Block or press
as described on the information page.
Join right shoulder seam using back stitch or
mattress stitch if preferred.

Neckband

With RS facing and using 3.25mm (US 3)
needles and A, pick up and knit 40 [40: 42:
44: 45] sts down left side of neck, 18 [18: 20:
20: 20] sts from front, 40 [40: 42: 44: 45] sts
up right side of neck, then 52 [54: 58: 60: 60]
sts from back. 150 [152: 162: 168: 170] sts.
Slip sts onto LH needle, thus having RS
facing for next row.

Change to C and knit 4 rows, ending with
RS facing for next row.

Change to B and knit 5 rows, ending with
WS facing for next row.

Cast off knitwise.

Join left shoulder and neckband seam.

Armhole borders (both alike)

With RS facing and using 3.25mm (US 3)
needles and A, pick up and knit 103 [114:
121: 131: 138] sts evenly all round armhole
edge.

Work as given for Neck band.

Cast off knitwise.

Sew Side Seams.

Using photo as a guide, stitch patch pocket
into place.

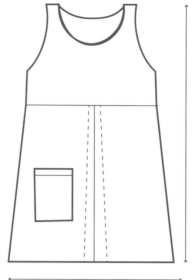

87 88: 90: 92: 94] cm
(34¼ [34¾: 35½: 36¼: 37] in)

46 [54: 57: 63: 67] cm
(18¼ [20½: 22½: 24½: 26½] in)

GARDEN SONG BLANKET

FINISHED SIZE

Blue Tit squares 40cm x 40cm (15¾in
x 15¾in) before seaming.
Sparrow and Birdy Footprint squares 20cm
x 20cm (8in x 8in) before seaming.
Completed Blanket 155.5cm (61¼in) wide
x 157.5cm (62in) long.

YARN

Rowan Felted Tweed DK

50g(1¾oz)/ 175m (191yds) balls

A Gilt 160	17 x 50g	
B Carbon 159	1 x 50g	
C Avocado 161	1 x 50g	
D Maritime 167	8 x 50g	
E Clay 177	1 x 50g	
F Mineral 181	1 x 50g	

NEEDLES

3.25mm (UK 10/US 3) circular needle,
150cm (60in) long
1 pair 3.75mm (UK 9/US 5) needles
Cable needle

TENSION

24 sts and 32 rows to 10cm/4in over st st
on 3.75mm (UK 9/US 5) needles.

SPECIAL ABBREVIATIONS

M1L = Make 1 left. Pick up loop between
last and next st from the front and knit into
the back of this loop.
M1R = Make 1 right. Pick up loop between
last and next st from behind and knit into
the front of this loop.
T2L = Slip 1 st to cable needle and hold at
front; p1; k1 from cable needle.
T2R = Slip 1 st to cable needle and hold at
back; k1; p1 from cable needle.

JONES SAYS

"This blue tit design is worked
using the intarsia technique,
however you can use the Fairisle
technique to strand across isolated
areas where there are only a few
stitches of a certain colour, such
as the bird's beak and wing stripe.
Where stranding, take extra care
to maintain an even tension. See
p 125 & 130 for our tutorials on
these techniques.

The blanket consists of individually
knitted squares that are then sewn
together before picking up and
knitting the edging.

The number of stitches in a row,
and the number of rows in a
square differ slightly in some
instances. Therefore, when sewing
pieces together, ease any extra
stitches or rows into the adjoining
seam.

Join squares by sewing cast off
edge of one square to cast on
edge of the next square to form
vertical strips, then sew the
strips together."

SQUARE A:
RIGHT FACING BLUE TIT – Make 2
Using 3.75mm (US 5) needles and yarn A cast on 95 sts. Beg with a K row, working in st st throughout and using the intarsia technique, work rows 1-128 of Chart A (on p 84), ending with RS facing for next row. Cast off.

SQUARE B:
LEFT FACING BLUE TIT– Make 2
Using 3.75mm (US 5) needles and yarn A cast on 95 sts. Beg with a K row, working in st st throughout and using the intarsia technique, work rows 1-128 Chart B (on p 85), ending with RS facing for next row. Cast off.

SQUARE C:
RIGHT FACING SPARROW –Make 14
Using 3.75mm (US 5) needles and yarn D cast on 48 sts. Beg with a K row, working in st st throughout and using the intarsia technique, work rows 1-64 of Chart C (on p 86), ending with RS facing for next row. Cast off.

SQUARE D:
LEFT FACING SPARROW– Make 14
Using 3.75mm (US 5) needles and yarn D cast on 48 sts. Beg with a K row, working in st st throughout and using the intarsia technique, work rows 1-64 of Chart D (on p 86), ending with RS facing for next row. Cast off.

SQUARE E: BIRDY FOOTPRINTS 1 – Make 10
Using 3.75mm (US 5) needles and yarn A cast on 48 sts.
Row 1: Purl.
Row 2: Knit.
Rows 3 to 6: As rows 1 and 2, twice.
Row 7: P40, k1, p to end.
Row 8: K7, p1, k to end.
Rows 9 and 10: As rows 7 and 8.
Row 11: P32, k1, p5, p2tog, MIR, k1, MIL, p2tog, p to end.

Row 12: K6, p3, k6, p1, k to end.
Row 13: P32, k1, p5, T2R, k1, T2L, p to end.
Row 14: K5, (p1, k1) twice, p1, k5, p1, k to end.
Row 15: P30, p2tog, MIR, k1, MIL, p2tog, p2, T2R, p1, k1, p1, T2L, p to end.
Row 16: K4, (p1, k2) twice, p1, k3, p3, k to end.
Row 17: P30, T2R, k1, T2L, p5, k1, p to end.
Row 18: K7, p1, k5, (p1, k1) twice, p1, k to end.
Row 19: P8, k1, p20, T2R, p1, k1, p1, T2L, p to end.
Row 20: K12, (p1, k2) twice, p1, k20, p1, k to end.
Row 21: P8, k1, p23, k1, p to end.
Row 22: K15, p1, k23, p1, k to end.
Row 23: P6, p2tog, MIR, k1, MIL, p2tog, p5, k1, p to end.
Row 24: K31, p1, k6, p3, k to end.
Row 25: P6, T2R, k1, T2L, p5, k1, p to end.
Row 26: K31, p1, k5, (p1, k1) twice, p1, k to end.
Row 27: P5, T2R, p1, k1, p1, T2L, p2, p2tog, MIR, k1, MIL, p2tog, p to end.
Row 28: K30, p3, k3, (p1, k2) twice, p1, k to end.
Row 29: P8, k1, p5, T2R, k1, T2L, p to end.
Row 30: K29, (p1, k1) twice, p1, k5, p1, k to end.
Row 31: P13, T2R, p1, k1, p1, T2L, p to end.
Row 32: K28, (p1, k2) twice, p1, k to end.
Row 33: P16, k1, p to end.
Row 34: K31, p1, k to end.
Beg with a P row work 10 rows in rev st st, ending with RS facing for next row.
Row 45: P21, k1, p to end.
Row 46: K26, p1, k to end.
Rows 47 and 48: As rows 45 and 46.
Row 49: P19, p2tog, MIR, k1, MIL, p2tog, p5, k1, p to end.
Row 50: K18, p1, k6, p3, k to end.
Row 51: P19, T2R, k1, T2L, p5, k1, p to end.
Row 52: K18, p1, k5, (p1, k1) twice, p1, k to end.
Row 53: P18, T2R, p1, k1, p1, T2L, p2, p2tog, MIR, k1, MIL, p2tog, p to end.
Row 54: K17, p3, k3, (p1, k2) twice, p1, k to

end.
Row 55: P21, k1, p5, T2R, k1, T2L, p to end.
Row 56: K16, (p1, k1) twice, p1, k5, p1, k to end.
Row 57: P26, T2R, p1, k1, p1, T2L, p to end.
Row 58: K15, (p1, k2) twice, p1, k to end.
Row 59: P29, k1, p to end.
Row 60: K18, p1, k to end.
Row 61: Purl.
Row 62: Knit.
Rows 63 and 64: As rows 61 and 62. Cast off.

SQUARE F: BIRDY FOOTPRINTS 2 – Make 10
Using 3.75mm (US 5) needles and yarn A cast on 48 sts.
Row 1: Purl.
Row 2: Knit.
Rows 3 to 6: As rows 1 and 2, twice.
Row 7: P7, k1, p to end.
Row 8: K to last 7 sts, p1, k to end.
Rows 9 and 10: As rows 7 and 8.
Row 11: P5, p2tog, MIR, k1, MIL, p2tog, p5, k1, p to end.
Row 12: K32, p1, k6, p3, k to end.
Row 13: P5, T2R, k1, T2L, p5, k1, p to end.
Row 14: K32, p1, k5, (p1, k1) twice, p1, k to end.
Row 15: P4, T2R, p1, k1, p1, T2L, p2, p2tog, MIR, k1, MIL, p2tog, p to end.
Row 16: K31, p3, k3, (p1, k2) twice, p1, k to end.
Row 17: P7, k1, p5, T2R, k1, T2L, p to end.
Row 18: K30, (p1, k1) twice, p1, k5, p1, k to end.
Row 19: P12, T2R, p1, k1, p1, T2L, p20, k1, p to end.
Row 20: K8, p1, k20, (p1, k2) twice, p1, k to end.
Row 21: P15, k1, p23, k1, p to end.
Row 22: K8, p1, k23, p1, k to end.
Row 23: P31, k1, p5, p2tog, MIR, k1, MIL, p2tog, p to end.
Row 24: K7, p3, k6, p1, k to end.
Row 25: P31, k1, p5, T2R, k1, T2L, p to end.
Row 26: K6, (p1, k1) twice, p1, k5, p1, k to end.

Row 27: P29, p2tog, M1R, k1, M1L, p2tog, p2, T2R, p1, k1, p1, T2L, p to end.

Row 28: K5, (p1, k2) twice, p1, k3, p3, k to end.

Row 29: P29, T2R, k1, T2L, p5, k1, p to end.

Row 30: K8, p1, k5, (p1, k1) twice, p1, k to end.

Row 31: P28, T2R, p1, k1, p1, T2L, p to end.

Row 32: K13, (p1, k2) twice, p1, k to end.

Row 33: P31, k1, p to end.

Row 34: K16, p1, k to end.

Beg with a P row work 10 rows in rev st st, ending with RS facing for next row.

Row 45: P26, k1, p to end.

Row 46: K21, p1, k to end.

Rows 47 and 48: As rows 45 and 46.

Row 49: P18, k1, p5, p2tog, M1R, k1, M1L, p2tog, p to end.

Row 50: K20, p3, k6, p1, k to end.

Row 51: P18, k1, p5, T2R, k1, T2L, p to end.

Row 52: K19, (p1, k1) twice, p1, k5, p1, k to end.

Row 53: P16, p2tog, M1R, k1, M1L, p2tog, p2, T2R, p1, k1, p1, T2L, p to end.

Row 54: K18, (p1, k2) twice, p1, k3, p3, k to end.

Row 55: P16, T2R, k1, T2L, p5, k1, p to end.

Row 56: K21, p1, k5, (p1, k1) twice, p1, k to end.

Row 57: P15, T2R, p1, k1, p1, T2L, p to end.

Row 58: K26, (p1, k2) twice, p1, k to end.

Row 59: P18, k1, p to end.

Row 60: K29, p1, k to end.

Row 61: Purl.

Row 62: Knit.

Rows 63 and 64: As rows 61 and 62.

Cast off.

MAKING UP

Weave in ends on wrong side of each square and block or press gently. Referring to the Layout diagram, join squares together using backstitch or mattress stitch if preferred.

Edging

With RS facing, using 3.25mm (US 3) circular needle and Yarn A, pick up and knit 384 sts along right hand edge of blanket.

Knit 7 rows increasing 1 st at each end of all **WS** rows, ending with RS facing for next row. 392 sts.

Picot cast off

Cast off 2 sts, *transfer st on right hand needle back onto left hand needle, cast on 2 sts, cast off 4 sts, rep from * to end.

Rep for left hand edge of blanket.

With RS facing and Yarn A, pick up and knit 370 sts along bottom edge of blanket.

Rep edging as for side edges above (note: you will have 378sts before cast off).

Rep for top edge of blanket.

Neatly slip stitch border edges together at each corner.

Cover edging with a damp ironing cloth and press very lightly.

LAYOUT DIAGRAM

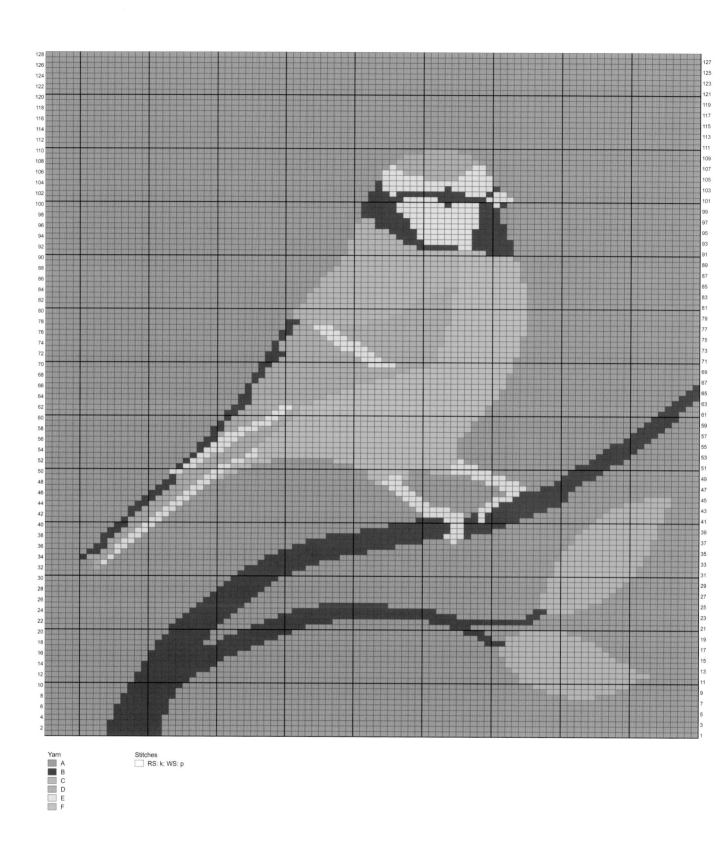

Yarn
- A
- B
- C
- D
- E
- F

Stitches
☐ RS: k; WS: p

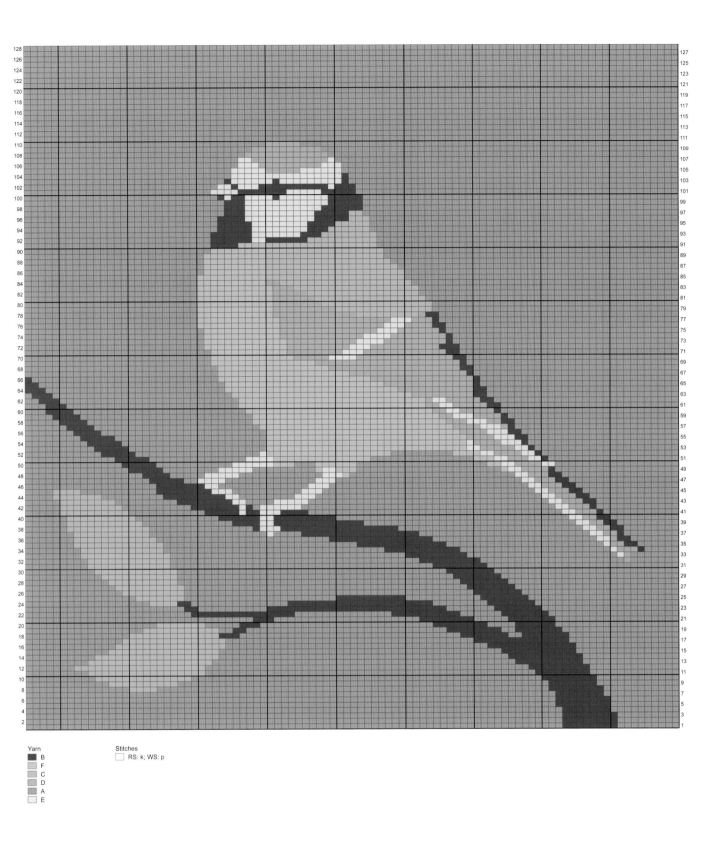

Yarn
■ B
▨ F
▨ C
▨ D
▨ A
□ E

Stitches
□ RS: k; WS: p

CHART C

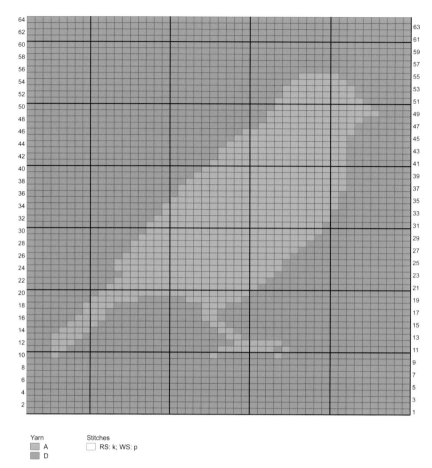

Yarn

◻ A
◼ D

Stitches

☐ RS: k; WS: p

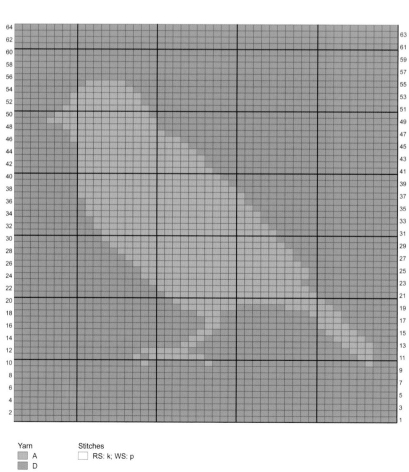

Yarn

◻ A
◼ D

Stitches

☐ RS: k; WS: p

GARDEN SONG CUSHION

FINISHED SIZE
39cm (15½in) x 39cm (15½in), designed to
fit cushion pad snugly.

YARN
Rowan Felted Tweed DK
50g(1¾oz)/ 175m (191yds) balls
A Gilt 160   3 x 50g
B Carbon 159   1 x 50g
C Avocado 161   1 x 50g
D Maritime 167   1 x 50g
E Clay 177   1 x 50g
F Mineral 181   1 x 50g

NEEDLES
1 pair 3mm (UK 11/US 2-3) needles
1 pair 3.75mm (UK 9/US 5) needles

BUTTONS
6 x 20-30mm (¾ -1in) buttons

OTHER
40cm (15¾in) x 40cm (15¾in) cushion pad

TENSION
24 sts and 32 rows to 10cm/4in over st
on 3.75mm (UK 9/US 5) needles.

SPECIAL ABBREVIATIONS
M1L = Make 1 left. Pick up loop between
last and next st from the front and knit into
the back of this loop.
M1R = Make 1 right. Pick up loop between
last and next st from behind and knit into
the front of this loop.
T2L = Slip 1 st to cable needle and hold at
front; p1; k1 from cable needle.
T2R = Slip 1 st to cable needle and hold at
back; k1; p1 from cable needle.

JONES SAYS
"If you are knitting the Garden
Song Blanket you will only need to
purchase yarn A as you will have
enough remaining yarns in the
other colours to complete
the cushion.

This blue tit design is worked using
the intarsia technique, however
you can use the Fairisle technique
to strand across isolated areas
where there are only a few
stitches of a certain colour, such
as the bird's beak and wing stripe.
Where stranding, take extra care
to maintain an even tension.
See pp 125 & 130 for our tutorials
on
these techniques.

You can choose between either a
left or right facing Blue Tit design
for your cushion front."

FRONT PANEL

Using 3.75mm (US 5) needles and yarn A cast on 95 sts. Beg with a knit row, working in st st throughout and using the intarsia technique (on page 125), work rows 1-128 of either Chart A or Chart B on p 84 & 85, placing a marker at each end of row 80, and ending with RS facing for next row.
Cast off.

LOWER BACK PANEL

With RS facing, using yarn A and 3mm (US 2-3) needles, pick up and knit 95 sts along cast on edge of cushion front.
Knit 1 row.
Change to 3.75mm (US 5) needles.
Next Row (RS): Purl.
Next Row (WS): Knit.

Bird foot pattern

Row 1: P7, k1, *p15, k1, rep from * to last 7 sts, p7.
Row 2: K7, p1, *k15, p1, rep from * to last 7 sts, k7.
Rows 3 and 4: As rows 1 and 2.
Row 5: P5, *p2tog, M1R, k1, M1L, p2tog, p11, rep from * to last 10 sts, p2tog, M1R, k1, M1L, p2tog, p5.
Row 6: K6, *p3, k13, rep from * to last 9 sts, p3, k6.
Row 7: P5, *T2R, k1, T2L, p11, rep from * to last 10 sts, T2R, k1, T2L, p5.
Row 8: K5, *(p1, k1) twice, p1, k11, rep from * to last 10 sts, (p1, k1) twice, p1, k5.
Row 9: P4, *T2R, p1, k1, p1, T2L, p9, rep from * to last 11 sts, T2R, p1, k1, p1, T2L, p4.
Row 10: K4, *(p1, k2) twice, p1, k9, rep from * to last 11 sts, (p1, k2) twice, p1, k4.
Row 11 and 12: As rows 1 and 2.
Row 13: Purl.
Row 14: Knit.
Row 15 & 16: As row 13 and 14.
Row 17: *P15, k1, rep from * to last 15 sts, p15.
Row 18: *K15, p1, rep from * to last 15 sts, k15.
Row 19 and 20: As rows 17 and 18.
Row 21: P13, *p2tog, M1R, k1, M1L, p2tog, p11, rep from * to last 2 sts, p2.
Row 22: K14, *p3, k13, rep from * to last st, k1.
Row 23: P13, *T2R, k1, T2L, p11, rep from * to last 2 sts, p2.
Row 24: K13, *(p1, k1) twice, p1, k11, rep from * to last 2 sts, k2.
Row 25: P12, *T2R, p1, k1, p1, T2L, p9, rep from * to last 3 sts, p3.
Row 26: K12, *(p1, k2) twice, p1, k9, rep from * to last 3 sts, k3.
Row 27 and 28: As rows 17 and 18.
Row 29: Purl.
Row 30: Knit.
Row 31 and 32: As row 29 and 30.
Rows 1-32 set bird foot pattern. Work these 32 rows once more, then repeat rows 1-12 thus ending on a RS facing for next row.
Place marker at each end of row.
Change to 3mm (US 2-3) needles.
Beg with a purl row, work 14 rows in reverse st st.
Knit 4 rows, ending with RS facing for next row.
Cast off.

UPPER BACK PANEL

With RS facing, using yarn A and 3mm (US 2-3) needles, pick up and knit 95 sts along cast off edge of cushion front.
Knit 1 row then change to 3.75mm (UK 9/US 5) needles.

Rib pattern

Row 1 (RS): *P7, k1, rep from * to last 7 sts, p7.
Row 2 (WS): *K7, p1, rep from * to last 7 sts, k7.
These 2 rows set rib pattern. Continue in rib pattern for a further 30 rows, ending with a RS facing for next row.

Buttonhole band

Change to 3mm (US 2-3) needles and knit 7 rows ending with WS facing for next row.
Row 1 (WS): K6, cast off next 3 sts, *k13, cast off 3 sts, rep from * to last 6 sts, k6.
Row 2 (RS): K6, *turn and cast on 3 sts, turn and k13, rep from * to last 6 sts, turn and cast on 3 sts, k6.

Knit 5 rows, dec 1 st at centre of final row and ending with a RS facing for next row. 94 sts.

Picot cast off

Cast off 2 sts, *transfer st on right hand needle back onto left hand needle, cast on 2 sts, cast off 4 sts, rep from * to end.

MAKING UP

Weave in ends on wrong side and block or press gently. Ensuring that the picot edging will line up with markers placed on front panel, sew side seams of upper back panel. Sew side seams of lower back panel to front, ensuring markers line up with edge of upper panel. Insert remaining lower panel under the finished edge of upper back panel and sew down in place. Sew buttons onto lower panel to correspond with buttonholes. Insert cushion pad.

LUMI BEADED LACE MITTENS

FINISHED SIZE

To fit average female hand approximately 20cm (8in) circumference above thumb (designed to fit snugly). 20.5cm (8¼in) in length when laid flat, after edges are sewn down.

YARN

Rowan Pure Wool Superwash DK
50g (1¾oz) 130m (142yd)
Damson 030   2 x 50g

NEEDLES

Set of 3.00mm (UK 11/US 2/3) DPNs
Set of 3.25mm (UK 10/US 3) DPNs

OTHER

100 Debbie Abrahams Beads, size 6, Amethyst, Code Ref: 41
3 stitch markers (see notes)
Large safety pin or length of waste yarn to hold thumb stitches

TENSION

40 stitches and 30 rows over 10cm (4in) measured over twisted rib worked in the round, on 3mm (UK 11/US 2/3) DPNs.

SPECIAL ABBREVIATIONS

M = marker to denote the beginning and end of rounds.
M1 = make 1 stitch: Pick up loop between last and next st from the front and knit into the back of this loop.
PB = place a bead on the next stitch (see notes on p 122).
STM1/2 = slip thumb marker 1/2
TM1 = thumb marker 1
TM2 = thumb marker 2

SMITH SAYS

"It is helpful to have 3 stitch markers which are different from each other – 1 colour for the main marker, another the thumb markers.

The pattern has a stretchy rib so one size fits all. However, I had 27g of yarn left over, so if you wished to lengthen the mittens with a few more rounds of rib, or an extra lace repeat, you would have enough wool, within reason. If you add lace repeats, you will need extra beads."

MITTENS (make 2 alike)

Thread on 50 beads (see notes on p 122).

Picot edge cuff

With 3mm needles cast on 50 sts.

Taking care not to twist cast on edge, place marker and work in rounds as follows:

Knit 8 rnds.

Change to 3.25mm needles.

Fold line: *Yfwd, k2tog, rep from * to end.

Knit 8 rnds.

Change to 3mm needles.

Next rnd: *K1tbl, p1, rep from * to end.

This rnd forms rib. Cont until rib section measures 5cm (2in).

Next rnd: (K2tog, k4) 7 times, k2tog, k to end. 42 sts.

Change to 3.25mm needles.

Next rnd: Knit.

Beaded lace section

Rnd 1: *K2tog, yfwd, k1, PB, k1, yfwd, skpo, rep from * to end.

Rnd 2: Knit.

Rnd 3: *K2tog, yfwd, k3, yfwd, skpo, rep from * to end.

Rnd 4: Knit.

These 4 Rnds form beaded lace patt. Rep rnds 1 – 4 twice more, then rnd 1 once more.

Thumb gusset section

Rnd 1: K17, place TM1, M1, k1, M1, place TM2, k to end. 44 sts.

Rnd 2: (K2tog, yfwd, k3, yfwd, skpo) twice, k2tog, yfwd, k1, STM1, k3, STM2, k1, yfwd, skpo, *k2tog, yfwd, k3, yfwd, skpo, rep from * to end.

Rnd 3: K17, STM1, M1, k3, M1, STM2, k to end. 46 sts.

Rnd 4: (K2tog, yfwd, k1, PB, k1, yfwd, skpo) twice, k2tog, yfwd, k1, STM1, k5, STM2, k1, yfwd, skpo, *k2tog, yfwd, k1, PB, k1, yfwd, skpo, rep from * to end.

These 4 rnds set pattern and thumb gusset shaping. Working shaping as set, work 12 rnds more. 58 sts.

Rnd 17: K to and remove TM1, sl next 17 sts onto holder, remove TM2, cast on 3 sts onto the RH needle, reach across the gap, k to end. 44 sts.

Rnd 18: (K2tog, yfwd, k3, yfwd, skpo) twice, k2tog, yfwd, k2tog, k1, k2tog, yfwd, skpo, *k2tog, yfwd, k3, yfwd, skpo, rep from * to end. 42 sts.

Rnd 19: Knit.

Resume beaded lace patt and work rnds 1 – 3 once more.

Change to 3mm needles.

Next rnd: (K9, kfb) 4 times, k2. 46 sts.

Work 6 rnds in Twisted Rib as at cuff.

Change to 3.25mm needles.

Knit 5 rnds.

Next rnd: *Yfwd, k2tog, rep from * to end.

Change to 3mm needles.

Knit 5 rnds.

Cast off loosely using a 3.25mm needle.

Thumb

With 3.25mm needles, sl the 17 sts on the holder onto 2 DPNs. Using a 3rd DPN, pick up and knit 5 sts over the area where you cast on the 3 sts earlier. Place M, and with 4th needle join to knit in the round. 22 sts.

Next rnd: K to last 5 sts, k2tog, k1, k2tog. 20 sts.

Knit 4 rnds.

Change to 3.00mm needles.

Work 4 rnds in Twisted Rib as at cuff.

Cast off in rib.

MAKING UP

Sew in ends. No need to block. Turn the mitten inside out. Fold the cuff and finger edges down at the picot fold-line and, taking care not to affect the tension/elasticity in the fit of the mitten, slip-stitch down on the **WS**.

COCKLESHELL CARDIGAN

FINISHED SIZE

	S	M	L	XL	XXL	
To fit Bust	81-86	91-97	102-107	112-117	122-127	cm
	32-34	36-38	40-42	44-46	48-50	in

YARN

Rowan Panama 50g (1¾oz)/ 135m (148yds) balls

Lotus 309	8	9	11	12	13	50g

NEEDLES

1 pair 2.75mm (UK 12/US 2) needles
1 pair 3.25mm (UK 10/US 3) needles

BUTTONS

15mm (½in) buttons × 5

TENSION

27 sts and 36 rows to 10cm/4in over st st
on 3.25mm (UK 10/US 3) needles.

SPECIAL ABBREVIATIONS

CL5 = cluster 5 thus: k5, slip successively the
2nd, 3rd, 4th, and 5th sts just worked over
the 1st st and off the needle.

JONES SAYS

"For best results use the thumb or
a long tail cast-on as this better
complements the shell edging."

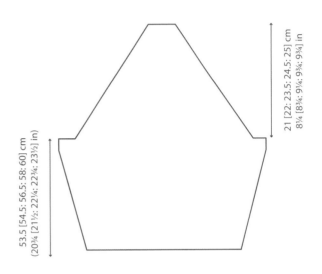

21 [22: 23.5: 24.5: 25] cm
8¼ [8¾: 9¼: 9¾: 9¾] in

53.5 [54.5: 56.5: 58: 60] cm
(20¾ [21½: 22¼: 22¾: 23½] in)

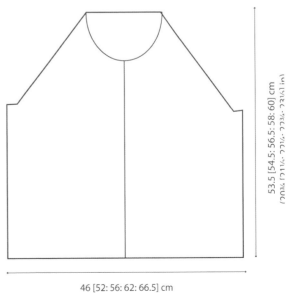

53.5 [54.5: 56.5: 58: 60] cm
(20¾ [21½: 22¼: 22¾: 23½] in)

46 [52: 56: 62: 66.5] cm
(18 [20½: 22: 24½: 26¼] in)

BACK

Using 3.25mm (US 3) needles cast on 159 [179: 194: 214: 229] sts.

Change to 2.75mm (US 2) needles and work edging as follows:

Row 1 (RS): K2, yfwd, * CL5, yfwd; rep from * to last 2 sts, k2. 67 [75: 81: 89: 95] sts.

Row 2: P2, *(p1, yrn, k1 tbl) into next st, p1; rep from * to last st, p1. 131 [147: 159: 175: 187] sts.

Row 3: K3, k1tbl, *k3, k1 tbl; rep from * to last 3 sts, k3.

Knit 2 rows.

Dec row: (WS): K49 [57: 63: 71: 77], k2tog, (k8, k2tog) 3 times, k to end. 127 [143: 155: 171:183] sts.

Change to 3.25mm (US 3) needles.

Row 7 (RS): Knit.

Row 8: Purl.

Row 9: K47 [55: 61: 69: 75], (yfrn, p1, p3tog, p1, yrn, k2) 5 times, k to end.

Row 10: Purl.

Rows 7-10 set pattern for back lace panel.

Work a further 10 rows as set, ending with RS facing for next row.

Dec 1 st at each end of next and 3 foll 24th rows. 119 [135: 147: 163: 175] sts.

Cont without shaping until work measures 29 [30: 30.5: 31: 32.5] cm (11½ [11¾: 12: 12¼: 12¾] in), ending with RS facing for next row.

Shape raglan

Cast off 4 [6: 8: 10: 12] sts at beg of next 2 rows. 111 [123: 131: 143: 151] sts.

Next Row (RS): K1, skpo, k to last 3 sts, k2tog, k1.

Next Row: (P1, p2tog) 0 [1: 1: 1: 1] times, p to last 0 [3: 3: 3: 3] sts, (p2tog tbl, p1) 0 [1: 1: 1: 1] times.

Dec 1 st as set at each end of next 1 [1: 3: 9: 11] rows, then on every foll alt row until 45 [43: 45: 47: 51] sts rem.

Size small only: Dec 1 st at each end of 2

foll 4th rows. 41 sts.

For all sizes

Work 1 row, ending with RS facing for next row.

Cast off rem sts.

LEFT FRONT

Using 3.25mm (size 3) needles cast on 79 [89: 94: 104: 114] sts.

Change to 2.75mm (US 2) needles and work edging as follows:

Row 1 (RS): K2, yfwd, * CL5, yfwd; rep from * to last 2 sts, k2. 35 [39: 41: 45: 49] sts.

Row 2: P2, *(p1, yfwd, k1 tbl) into next st, p1; rep from * to last st. p1. 67 [75: 79: 87: 95] sts.

Row 3: K3, k1tbl, *k3, k1 tbl; rep from * to last 3 sts, k3.

Knit 2 rows.

Dec row (WS): K to last 16 sts, k4, k2tog, k8, k2tog. 65 [73: 77: 85: 93] sts.

Change to 3.25mm (US 3) needles.

Row 7 (RS): Knit.

Row 8: Purl.

Row 9: K to last 14 [14: 14: 14: 17] sts, (yfrn, p1, p3tog, p1, yfwd, k2) twice, k0 [0: 0: 0: 3].

Row 10: Purl.

Rows 7-10 set pattern for front lace panel.

Work a further 10 rows as set, ending with RS facing for next row.

Dec 1 st at beg of next and 3 foll 24th rows. 61 [69: 73: 81: 89] sts.

Cont without shaping until work measures 29 [30: 30.5: 31: 32.5] cm (11½ [11¾: 12: 12¼: 12¾] in), ending with RS facing for next row.

Shape raglan

Next row (RS): Cast off 4 [6: 8: 10: 12] sts at beg of next row. 57 [63: 65: 71: 77] sts.

Work 1 row.

Next row (RS): K1, skpo, patt to end.

Next row: Patt to last 0 [3: 3: 3: 3] sts, (p2tog tbl, p1) 0 [1: 1: 1: 1] times.

Dec 1 st as set at raglan edge of next 1 [1: 3: 9: 11] rows, then on every foll alt row until

37 [40: 41: 42: 47] sts rem, ending with WS facing for next row.

Shape Front neck

Next row (WS): Cast off 5 [6: 5: 6: 7] sts, patt to end. 32 [34: 36: 36: 40] sts.

Dec 1 st at raglan edge as set at beg of next and 12 [16:18:18:19] foll alt rows then on 2 [0:0:0:0] foll 4th rows and AT SAME TIME dec 1 st at neck edge of next 7 [7:7:5:9] rows, 5 [5:3:4:5] foll alt rows, then on 3 [3:5:6:4] foll 4th row. 2 sts.

Work 1 row, ending with RS facing for next row.

Next row: K2tog. Fasten off.

RIGHT FRONT

Using 3.25mm (size 3) needles cast on 79 [89: 94: 104: 114] sts.

Change to 2.75mm (US 2) needles and work edging as follows:

Row 1 (RS): K2, yfwd, * CL5, yfwd; rep from * to last 2 sts, k2. 35 [39: 41: 45: 49] sts.

Row 2: P2, *(p1, yfwd, k1 tbl) into next st, p1; rep from * to last st. p1. 67 [75: 79: 87: 95] sts.

Row 3: K3, k1tbl, *k3, k1 tbl; rep from * to last 3 sts, k3.

Knit 2 rows.

Dec row (WS): K4, k2tog, k8, k2tog, k to end. 65 [73: 77: 85: 93] sts.

Change to 3.25mm (US 3) needles.

Row 7 (RS): Knit.

Row 8: Purl.

Row 9: K2 [2: 2: 2: 5], (yfrn, p1, p3tog, p1, yfwd, k2) twice, k to end.

Row 10: Purl.

Rows 7-10 set pattern for back lace panel.

Work a further 10 rows as set, ending with RS facing for next row.

Dec 1 st at end of next and 3 foll 24th rows. 61 [69: 73: 81: 89] sts.

Cont without shaping until work measures 29 [30: 30.5: 31: 32.5] cm (11½ [11¾: 12: 12¼: 12¾] in), ending with WS facing for next row.

Shape raglan

Next row (WS): Cast off 4 [6: 8: 10: 12] sts at beg of next row. 57 [63: 65: 71: 77] sts.

Next row (RS): Patt to last 3 sts, k2tog, K1.

Next row (WS): (P1, p2tog tbl) 0 [1: 1: 1: 1] times, patt to end.

Dec 1 st as set at raglan edge of next 1 [1: 3: 9: 11] rows, then on every foll alt row until 37 [40: 41: 42: 47] sts rem.

Work 1 row, ending with RS facing for next row.

Shape Front neck

Next row (RS): Cast off 5 [6: 5: 6: 7] sts, patt to last 3 sts, k2tog, k1. 31 [33: 35: 35: 39] sts.

Dec 1 st at neck edge of next 7 [7:7:5:9] rows, 5 [5:3:4:5] foll alt rows, then on 3 [3:5:6:4] foll 4th row and AT SAME TIME dec 1 st at raglan edge as set at beg of next and 12 [16:18:18:19] foll alt rows then on 2 [0:0:0:0] foll 4th rows. 2 sts.

Work 1 row, ending with RS facing for next row.

Next row: K2tog. Fasten off.

SLEEVES

Using 3.25mm (size 3) needles cast on 89 [99: 109: 119: 129] sts.

Change to 2.75mm (US 2) needles and work edging as follows:

Row 1 (RS): K2, yfwd, * CL5, yfwd; rep from * to last 2 sts, k2. 39 [43: 47: 51: 55] sts.

Row 2: P2, *[p1, yfwd, k1 tbl] into next st, p1; rep from * to last st. p1.
75 [83: 91: 99: 107] sts.

Row 3: K3, k1tbl, *k3, k1 tbl; rep from * to last 3 sts, k3.

Knit 3 rows.

Change to 3.25mm (US 3) needles.

Row 7 (RS): Knit.

Row 8: Purl.

Row 9: K35 [39: 43: 47: 51], yfrn, p1, p3tog, p1, yfwd, k to end.

Row 10: Purl.

Rows 7-10 set pattern for sleeve lace panel.

Working in patt as set, inc 1 st at each end of 5th [3rd :3rd :3rd: 3rd] row and 3 [7: 7: 3: 5] foll 8th [6th: 6th: 6th: 6th] rows, then on every foll 6th [4th : 4th :4th : 4th] row to 91 [105: 115: 129: 137] sts.

Cont without shaping until work measures 20 [21: 22: 23: 24] cm (7¾ [8¼: 8¾: 9: 9½] in), ending with RS facing for next row.

Shape raglan

Cast off 4 [6: 8: 10: 12] sts at beg of next 2 rows. 83 [93: 99: 109: 113] sts.

Next row (RS): K1, skpo, k to last 3 sts, p2tog, k1.

Next row: (P1, p2tog) 0 [1: 1: 1: 1] times, p to last 0 [3: 3: 3: 3] sts, (p2tog tbl, p1) 0 [1: 1: 1: 1] times.

Working all raglan armhole decreases as set by last 2 rows, dec 1 st at each end of next 1 [1: 3: 9: 11] rows, then on every foll alt row until 17 [13: 13: 13: 13] sts rem.

Size small only

Dec 1 st at each end of 2 foll 4th rows. 13 sts.

For all sizes

Work 1 row, ending with RS facing for next row.

Cast off rem sts.

MAKING UP

Sew in ends and block or press as described on p 118.

Join raglan, sleeve and side seams using mattress stitch or back stitch if preferred.

Button band

With RS facing and using 2.75mm (US 2) needles, pick up and knit 112 [118: 119: 124: 128] sts evenly down left front opening edge, from neck shaping to cast-on edge.

Knit 8 rows, ending with **WS** facing for next row.

Cast off knitwise.

Buttonhole band

With RS facing and using 2.75mm (US 2) needles, pick up and knit 112 [118: 119: 124: 128] sts evenly up right front opening edge, from cast-on edge to neck shaping.

Knit 3 rows, ending with RS facing for next row.

Row 4 (RS): K66 [68: 69: 70: 74], *yfwd, k2tog, k10 [11: 11: 12: 12], rep from * twice more, yfwd, k2tog, k8 [9: 9: 10: 10].

Knit 4 rows, ending with **WS** facing for next row.

Cast off knitwise.

Neckband

With RS facing and using 2.75mm (US 2) needles, beg and ending at front opening edges, pick up and knit 33 [36: 38: 39: 42] sts up right front neck, 13 sts across sleeve top, 41 [43: 45: 47: 51] sts across back neck, 13 sts across top sleeve, and 33 [36: 38: 39: 42] sts down left front neck. 133 [141: 147: 151: 161] sts.

Knit 3 rows, ending with RS facing for next row.

Row 4 (RS): K3, yfwd, k2tog, k to end.

Knit 4 rows, ending with **WS** facing for next row.

Cast off knitwise.

Sew in all ends and attach buttons to correspond with buttonholes.

COASTAL BED RUNNER

FINISHED SIZE
140cm (55in) x 50cm (19½in). Fits across a single bed with generous overhang.

YARN
Rowan Purelife Revive

50g (1¾oz)/ 125m (137yds) balls

A Rock 465	1 x 50g
B Pearl 479	1 x 50g
C Basalt 462	1 x 50g
D Granite 464	1 x 50g
F Grit 473	2 x 50g
J Flint 469	1 x 50g
K Marble 466	1 x 50g

Rowan Creative Linen

100g (3½oz)/ 200m (219yds) skeins

E Natural 621	1 x 100g
G Darkness 636	1 x 100g
H Stormy 635	1 x 100g
I Cloud 620	1 x 100g

NEEDLES
3.25mm (UK 10/US 3) circular needle, 80 or 100cm (32 or 40in) long

4mm (UK 8/US 6) circular needle, 80 or 100cm (32 or 40in) long

TENSION
22 sts and 30 rows to 10cm (4in) over st st on 4mm (UK 8/US 6) needles.

JONES SAYS
"For best results use the thumb or a long tail cast-on as this better complements the garter st edging."

RUNNER

Using 3.25mm (US 3) circular needle and
yarn A cast on 308 sts and work in rows as
follows:

Rows 1 to 6: Knit.

Change to 4mm (US 6) needle and using
yarn B.

Row 7 (RS): K to end.

Row 8 (WS): K4, p to last 4 sts, k4.

These 2 rows set stocking stitch pattern
with garter stitch borders.

Cont in patt changing colours for stripe
sequence as folls:

Rows 9 and 10:Yarn B.

Rows 11 and 12:Yarn C.

Rows 13 and 14:Yarn B.

Rows 15 and 16:Yarn A.

Rows 17 and 18:Yarn B.

Rows 19 and 20:Yarn C.

Rows 21 and 22:Yarn A.

Rows 23 and 24: Yarn C.

Rows 25 to 28:Yarn D.

Rows 29 to 34:Yarn A.

Rows 35 and 36: Yarn E.

Rows 37 and 38:Yarn D.

Rows 39 and 40:Yarn E.

Rows 41 and 42:Yarn D.

Rows 43 to 48:Yarn E.

Rows 49 and 50:Yarn F.

Rows 51 and 52: Yarn E.

Rows 53 to 62:Yarn F.

Rows 63 and 64:Yarn G.

Rows 65 to 70:Yarn F.

Rows 71 and 72:Yarn G.

Rows 73 to 76:Yarn F.

Rows 77 and 78:Yarn G.

Rows 79 to 82:Yarn F.

Rows 83 to 86:Yarn G.

Rows 87 and 88:Yarn F.

Rows 89 to 96:Yarn G.

Rows 97 and 98:Yarn H.

Rows 99 and 100:Yarn G.

Rows 101 to 106:Yarn H.

Rows 107 and 108:Yarn I.

Rows 109 and 110:Yarn J.

Rows 111 and 112:Yarn I.

Rows 113 to 116:Yarn J.

Rows 117 and 118: Yarn I.

Rows 119 to 122:Yarn J.

Rows 123 to 126:Yarn I.

Rows 127 and 128:Yarn K.

Rows 129 and 130:Yarn I.

Rows 131 to 134:Yarn K.

Rows 135 and 136:Yarn I.

Rows 137 to 140: Yarn K.

Rows 141 and 142:Yarn I.

Row 143 to 145:Yarn K.

Change to 3.25mm (US 3) needles and knit
6 rows, ending with WS facing for next row.
Cast off knitwise.

MAKING UP

Weave in all ends, block or press gently.

COASTAL CUSHION

FINISHED SIZE
49.5cm (19½in) x 49.5cm (19½in), designed
to fit cushion pad snugly.

YARN
Rowan Purelife Revive 50g
(1¾oz)/ 125m (137yds) balls
A Rock 465   1 x 50g
B Pearl 479   1 x 50g
C Basalt 462   1 x 50g
D Granite 464   1 x 50g
F Grit 473   1 x 50g
J Flint 469   1 x 50g
K Marble 466   1 x 50g
Rowan Creative Linen 100g
(3½oz)/ 200m (219yds) skeins
E Natural 621   3 x 100g
G Darkness 636   1 x 100g
H Stormy 635   1 x 100g
I Cloud 620   1 x 100g

NEEDLES
1 pair 3.25mm (UK 10/US 3) needles
1 pair 4mm (UK 8/US 6) needles

OTHER
5 x 20-30mm (¾-1in) buttons
(see resources p 131)
50cm (19¾in) x 50cm (19¾in) cushion pad

TENSION
22 sts and 30 rows to 10cm (4in) over st st
on 4mm (UK 8/US 6) needles.

JONES SAYS
"If you are also knitting the Coastal
Runner you will only need to
purchase yarns A, F, & K and only 2
skeins of E as you will have enough
remaining yarns in the other
colours to complete the cushion."

FRONT

Using 4mm needles and yarn A cast on 109 sts.

Beg with a K row, working in st st throughout and changing colours for stripe sequence as folls:

Rows 1 to 6:Yarn A.

Rows 7 to 10:Yarn B.

Rows 11 and 12:Yarn C.

Rows 13 and 14:Yarn B.

Rows 15 and 16:Yarn A.

Rows 17 and 18:Yarn B.

Rows 19 and 20:Yarn C.

Rows 21 and 22:Yarn A.

Rows 23 and 24:Yarn C.

Rows 25 to 28:Yarn D.

Rows 29 to 34:Yarn A.

Rows 35 and 36:Yarn E.

Rows 37 and 38:Yarn D.

Rows 39 and 40:Yarn E.

Rows 41 and 42:Yyarn D.

Rows 43 to 48:Yarn E.

Rows 49 and 50:Yarn F.

Rows 51 and 52:Yarn E.

Rows 53 to 62:Yarn F.

Rows 63 and 64:Yarn G.

Rows 65 to 70:Yarn F.

Rows 71 and 72:Yarn G.

Rows 73 to 76:Yarn F.

Rows 77 and 78:Yarn G.

Rows 79 to 82:Yarn F.

Rows 83 to 86:Yarn G.

Rows 87 and 88:Yarn F, placing marker on each end of row 87.

Rows 89 to 96:Yarn G.

Rows 97 and 98:Yarn H.

Rows 99 and 100:Yarn G.

Rows 101 to 106:Yarn H.

Rows 107 and 108:Yarn I.

Rows 109 and 110:Yarn J.

Rows 111 and 112:Yarn I.

Rows 113 to 116:Yarn J.

Rows 117 and 118:Yarn I.

Rows 119 to 122:Yarn J.

Rows 123 to 126:Yarn I.

Rows 127 and 128:Yarn K.

Rows 129 and 130:Yarn I.

Rows 131 to 134:Yarn K.

Rows 135 and 136:Yarn I.

Rows 137 to 140:Yarn K.

Rows 141 and 142:Yarn I.

Row 143 to 150:Yarn K.

Cast off.

UPPER BACK PANEL (with Buttonholes)

Using 3.25mm (US 3) needles and yarn E pick up and knit 109 sts across cast off edge of front.

**Next row: Knit.

Change to 4mm (US 6) needles.

Rippled sand pattern

Row 1 (RS): K1, *p2, k1, rep from * to end.

Row 2 (WS): K3, *p1, k2, rep from * to last st, k1.

Row 3: K2, *p2, k1, rep from * to last 2 sts, p1, k1.

Row 4: K2, *p1, k2, rep from * to last 2 sts, p1, k1.

Row 5: K1, p1, *k1, p2, rep from * to last 2 sts, k2.

Row 6: K1, *p1, k2, rep from * to end.

Rows 7 to 10: As rows 1 to 4.

Rows 11 and 12: As rows 1 and 2.

Rows 13 and 14: As rows 5 and 6.

Rows 15 and 16: As rows 3 and 4.

These 16 rows form rippled sand pattern.** Repeat rows 1-16 twice, then work rows 1-15 once more, ending with a **WS** facing for next row.

Buttonhole band

Change to 3.25mm (US 3) needles.

Work garter stitch buttonhole band as follows:

Row 1 to 4: Knit.

Row 5 (WS): K7, cast off 3 sts, *k19 (20 sts on RH needle), cast off 3 sts, rep from * to last 6 sts, k6.

Row 6 (RS): K7, turn work and cast on 3 sts, turn work back again and *k20, turn work and cast on 3sts, turn work back again, rep from * to last 7 sts, k7.

Row 7 to 10: Knit, ending with **WS** facing for next row.

Cast off knitwise.

LOWER BACK PANEL

Using 3.25mm (US 3) needles and yarn E pick up and knit 109 sts across cast on edge of front panel.

Work as for Upper Back Panel from ** to **.

Rep these 16 rows a further 4 times.

Change to 3.25mm (US 3) needles and work rows 1-16 once more.

Cast off knitwise.

MAKING UP

Weave in ends and block or press gently. Sew side seams of upper back panel (with buttonholes) to front ensuring that the point where rippled sand pattern changes to garter stitch buttonhole band is in line with markers placed on front panel. Sew side seams of lower back panel to front, inserting cast off edge under the finished edge of upper back panel, and sew down in place. Sew buttons onto button band to correspond with buttonholes.

BOREAL CAPELET

FINISHED SIZE

Capelet measures 41cm (16in) deep from neck to cast off edge of border and 247cm (97¼in) wide along the bottom of the main section.

YARN

Rowan Chenille
50g (1¾oz)/110m (120yd) balls
A Midnight 760   7 x 50g
Rowan Finest
25g (1oz)/87m (95yd) balls
B Star 069   3 x 25g

NEEDLES

1 pair 4mm (UK 8/US 6) needles
2 x 4mm (UK 8/US 6) fixed cable circular needles, 120cm (47in) long or longer
2 x 3.75mm (UK 9/US 5) fixed cable circular needles, 120cm (47in) long

TENSION

19 sts and 32 rows to 10cm (4in) over st st using yarn A on 4.00mm (UK 8/US 6) needles.

SPECIAL ABBREVIATIONS

M1 = Make 1: Pick up loop between last and next st from behind and knit into the front of this loop.
M1P = Make 1 purlwise: Pick up loop between last and next st from behind and purl into the front of this loop.
M/PM/SM = marker/place marker/slip marker.

SMITH SAYS

"The capelet is knitted flat throughout.

The capelet can be started with the shorter 4mm (US 6) needles. As the number of stitches increases, change to a single fixed cable circular needle, and introduce the second fixed cable circular needle as the number of stitches increases further. For the border you will be using both circular needles throughout.

When picking up and knitting for the border around the bottom edge I used the 'bumps' in the fold line to pick up from. If you find you are a few short of, or over 468 stitches, and assuming it is not out by many, you can adjust this number on the next row."

CAPELET

With 4mm (US 6) needles and A, cast on 80 sts.

Knit 6 rows to form garter st neckband.

Next row (RS): K3, PM, M1, *k14, M1, PM, k1, PM, M1, rep from * to last 17 sts, k14, m1, PM, k3. 90 sts.

Next row (WS): K3, p to last 3 sts, slipping Ms as you pass them, k3.

Next row: Knit, slipping Ms as you pass them.

Next row: As last WS row.

Main Pattern

Row 1: K3, SM, M1, * k to next M, M1, SM, k1, SM, M1, rep from * to last 19 sts, k to next M, M1, SM, k3. 100 sts.

Row 2 (and all WS rows): K3, p to last 3 sts, slipping Ms as you pass them k3.

Row 3: Knit, slipping Ms as you pass them.

Row 4: As row 2.

These 4 rows set increases.

Inc as set on next and every foll 4th row to 210 sts, then on every foll alt row to 470 sts, swapping to longer needle/s as necessary. Work 1 row, ending with RS facing for next row.

Next row (RS): Knit.

Next row: K3, p to last 3 sts, k3.

Rep last 2 rows once more.

Next row: Knit.

Next row (WS): Knit to form fold line.

Next row: Knit.

Next row: Purl.

Rep last 2 rows once more. Cast off.

MAKING UP

Sew in ends. With WS facing, fold the bottom of the cape at the fold line and slip st the hem into place taking care not to pull or tighten the edge.

With WS facing, pin the capelet out, cover with a fine cloth and spray lightly with water. Refer to ball bands for instructions. With iron set to cool, skim over the cloth taking care not to press down especially at the sewn fold line. Remove cloth. Allow to dry before unpinning.

Border

With RS facing, using 3.75mm (US 5) circular needle and yarn B, pick up and knit 468 sts along the bottom of the capelet.

Next row: Purl.

Main Pleated Border Pattern

Row 1 (RS): *K6, M1P, rep from * to last 6 sts, k6. 545 sts.

Row 2: Knit the k sts and purl the p sts as they present themselves.

Row 3 and 4: As row 2.

Row 5: *K6, p1, M1P, rep from * to last 6 sts, k6. 622 sts.

Rows 6 to 8: As row 2.

Row 9: *K6, p2, M1P, rep from * to last 6 sts, k6. 699 sts.

Rows 10 to 12: As row 2.

Row 13: *K6, p3, M1P, rep from * to last 6 sts, k6. 776 sts.

Rows 14 to 16: As row 2.

Row 17: *K6, p4, M1P, rep from * to last 6 sts, k6. 853 sts.

Rows 18 to 20: As row 2.

Row 21: *K6, p5, M1P, rep from * to last 6 sts, k6. 930 sts.

Rows 22 to 24: As row 2.

Cast off in pattern.

Sew in ends. With WS facing, pin the border area of the capelet down (you may need to do this in sections) allowing purl sts to form pleats and cover with a fine cloth and lightly spray with water. Refer to ball band for instructions. With iron set to cool, lightly skim the work, taking care not to press down on the 'pleats'. Remove cloth and allow to dry before unpinning. Sew clasp or ribbons at front neck.

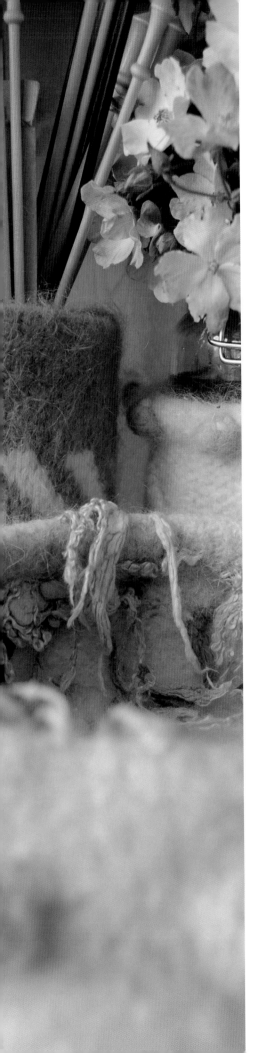

NEST
THREE FELTED BOWLS & CONTAINERS

This is a collection of three felted bowls and containers, each using a different technique or colour feature. There is a large shallow bowl which uses some simple Shibori felting embellishments. There is a smaller, rounded jar cover featuring a swirling colour pattern. And a larger felted cover, with fat cables and plump knitted bobbles, which fits a Kilner jar. None of the knitting is at all difficult.

The bowl is sturdy enough to fill with jewel-bright fruits, chocolate eggs, or pretty balls of yarn. The other containers bring a breath of spring to pots and jars, to show off your needles or a bunch of spring flowers.

SMITH SAYS

"Items were felted at 60 degrees in the washing machine, using a 60 minute cycle. If your 60 degree cycle is longer, stop the washing after 50 minutes and then switch to brief rinse/spin cycle mode.

Shape the items as soon as they come out of the wash. I put mine over a ceramic bowl or jars of approximately the same size as my desired finished dimensions and left them to dry.

This makes very dense and thick felt. If your felted bowl is not thick, is not approximately the size given above after felting, and you can still see the knitted texture of the fabric, consider re-felting it at 40 degrees. If you are going to do this, do not remove the marbles.

I use no fabric conditioner, just normal washing powder, tablets or liquid. Add a Colour Catcher sheet if you are using bright/dark coloured yarns. Add a couple of old tea-towels to the wash to add a bit of friction. I do not tie the felting in a bag or pillow case."

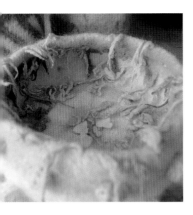

LARGE SHIBORI FELTED BOWL

FINISHED SIZE

Approx 11cm (4½in) in height laid flat and measured from cast on edge to cast off at base; top circumference of 60cm (23½in) **after** felting

YARN

Rowan Kid Classic

50g (1¾oz) /140m (153yds) balls

A Drought 876   2 x 50g

B Feather 828   1 x 50g

NEEDLES

7mm (UK 2/US 10 ½) fixed cable circular needle, 40cm (16in) long

Set of 7mm (UK 2/US 10 ½) DPNs

OTHER

Stitch marker

24 glass marbles size 14 – 17mm (1 – 1 ½in) (see notes on resources p 131)

Lengths of silk fibres to weave through the knitting (see notes on resources p 131)

Crochet hook to pull silks through the knitting

Lengths of fine string or 4 ply cotton yarn to tie in the marbles

TENSION

12 sts and 16 rows over 10cm/4in over st st worked in the round, using Kid Classic held double on 7mm (UK 2/US 10½) needles **before** felting.

SMITH SAYS

"Refer to shibori techniques on page 124 for further information on how to tie in marbles and weave in silk.

Make sure you tie the marbles into place using a non-felting thread. I use 4 ply cotton or fine string.

Remove the marbles as soon as it is done. If you leave them in place to dry, you may struggle to get them out."

BOWL

Yarn is held double throughout. Using 7mm (US 10½) circular needle, cast on 90 sts with yarn A. Taking care not to twist cast on edge, join to knit in the round and place marker.

Knit 5 rnds.

Next rnd: Purl (forms fold-line).

Knit 5 rnds.

Rnd 1: *K9, kfb, rep from * to end. 99 sts.

Rnd 2: Kfb, k to end. 100 sts.

Knit 2 rnds.

Rnd 5: *K9, kfb, rep from * to end. 110 sts.

Knit 2 rnds.

Change to yarn B.

Rnd 8: *K10, kfb, rep from * to end. 120 sts.

Knit 5 rnds.

Rnd 14: *K9, kfb, rep from * to end. 132 sts.

Knit 5 rnds.

Rnd 20: *K9, k2tog, rep from * to end. 120 sts.

Knit 5 rnds.

Rnd 26: *K8, k2tog, rep from * to end. 108 sts.

Rnd 27: Knit.

Change to yarn A.

Next rnd: Knit.

Base Section

Rnd 1: K4, *k2tog, k9, rep from * to last 5 sts, k2tog, k3. 98sts.

Rnd 2: Knit.

Rnd 3: K4, *k2tog, k9, rep from * to last 6 sts, k2tog, k4. 89 sts.

Change to yarn B. (Note: at some point in the next few rnds, you will have too few sts for the single needle, so when you wish, transfer sts to the DPNs and cont on these).

Rnd 4: Knit.

Rnd 5: K6, *k2tog, k9, rep from * to last 6 sts, k2tog, k4. 81 sts.

Rnd 6: Knit.

Rnd 7: K5, *k2tog, k8, rep from * to last 6 sts, k2tog, k4. 73 sts.

Rnd 8: Knit.

Rnd 9: K6, *k2tog, k8, rep from * to to last 7 sts, k2tog, k5. 66 sts.

Rnd 10: Knit.

Rnd 11: *K4, k2tog, rep from * to end. 55 sts.

Rnd 12: Knit.

Rnd 13: *K3, k2tog, rep from * to end. 44 sts.

Change to yarn A.

Rnd 14: *K3, k2tog, rep from * to last 4 sts. 36 sts.

Rnd 15: *K2tog, rep from * to end. 18 sts.

Rnd 16: *K2tog, rep from * to end. 9 sts.

Cut yarn leaving 20cm (8in) tail. Thread tail in a sewing up needle and pass yarn through the live sts, slipping them from the needles as you go. Draw to close and secure by sewing in end.

Turn bowl inside out. Fold the top brim down inside at the fold line (which will therefore now be the top rim of the bowl), and slip st into place, making sure not to pull the yarn too tight. Sew in all ends.

Using a crochet hook, weave lengths of silk through on the inside of the bowl. I focused on the areas where there was a colour change. Using photograph as a guide, tie in marbles in two staggered rows along the top two 'stripes' but avoiding the folded area right at the top. Cut off the ends of the tying thread so there is no more than about 3cm

(1¼in) left loose.

Wash at 60 degrees for approx 60 minutes. Once done, carefully remove marbles and pop the 'bumps' back into shape. Pull the bowl into shape whilst damp or stretch it over a bowl of similar shape and size to dry.

MEDIUM SPIRAL-COLOUR JAR-HOLDER

FINISHED SIZE
Approx 16cm (6¼in) in height; top circumference of 40cm (15¾in) **after** felting

YARN
Rowan Kid Classic
50g (1¾oz) /140m (153yds) balls
A Grasshopper 886   1 x 50g
B Feather 828   1 x 50g

NEEDLES
Set of 7mm (UK 2/US 10 ½) DPNs

OTHER
Stitch marker

TENSION
12 sts and 16 rows over 10cm/4in over stocking stitch worked in the round, using Kid Classic held double on 7mm (UK 2/US 10½) needles **before** felting.

SMITH SAYS
"See p 129 for further information about how to knit in the round on DPNs."

JAR-HOLDER
Yarn is held DOUBLE throughout. Using 7mm (US 10½) DPNs and yarn A, cast on 45 sts and arrange as evenly as possible between 3 needles. Taking care not to twist cast on edge, join to knit in the round and place stitch marker.
Knit 5 rnds.
Next rnd: Purl.
Knit 5 rnds.

Main jar-cover
Rnd 1: *K4, kfb, rep from * to end. 54 sts.
Rnd 2: Knit.
Rnd 3: K53, kfb . 55 sts.
Rnd 4: *K4, kfb, rep from * to end. 66 sts.
Rnd 5: Knit.
Rnd 6: K76, kfb. 78 sts.
Rnd 7: *K3 with yarn A, k3 with yarn B, rep from * to end.
Rnd 8: K2 with yarn A, *k3 with yarn B, k3 with yarn A, rep from * to last 4 sts, k3 with yarn B, k1 with yarn A.
Rnd 9: K1 with yarn A, *k3 with yarn B, k3 with yarn A, rep from * to last 5 sts, k3 with yarn B, k2 with yarn A.
Rnd 10: *K3 with yarn B, k3 with yarn A, rep from * to end.
Rnd 11: K2 with yarn B, *k3 with yarn A, k3 with yarn B, rep from * to last 4 sts, k3 with yarn A, k1 with yarn B.
Rnd 12: K1 with yarn B, *k3 with yarn A, k3 with yarn B, rep from * to last 5 sts, k3 with yarn A, k2 with yarn B.
Rnds 7-12 form spiralling colour patt.
Continue in patt until work measures 20cm (8in) from cast on edge.

Base Section
Break off yarn A and cont in yarn B only.
Rnd 1: K2 tog, k to end. 76 sts.
Rnd 2: *K2, k2tog, rep from * to end .57 sts.

Rnd 3: As rnd 1. 56 sts.
Rnd 4: As rnd 2. 42 sts.
Rnd 5: *K2tog, rep from * to end. 21 sts.
Rnd 6: K1, *k2tog, rep from * to end. 11 sts.
Rnd 7: As rnd 6. 6 sts.
Cut yarn leaving 20 cm (8 inch) tail. Thread tail in a sewing up needle and pass yarn through the live sts, slipping them from the needles as you go. Draw to close and secure by sewing in end.
Turn bowl inside out. Fold the top brim down at the fold line (which will therefore now be the top rim of the bowl), and slip st into place, making sure not to pull the yarn too tight. Sew in all ends.
Wash at 60 degrees for approx 60 minutes (see notes). Once done and while still damp, pull the bowl into shape and fit over the container you want it to cover – I used a stone pot. Dry fully with the pot or jar in place.

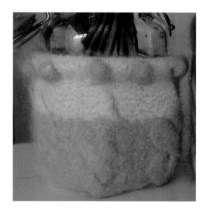

CABLED KILNER JAR COVER

FINISHED SIZE
Approx 14cm (5½) in height & top circumference of 46cm (18in) after felting
YARN
Rowan Kid Classic
50g (1¾ oz) /140m (153yds) balls
A Feather 828   1 x 50g
B Water 883   1 x 50g

NEEDLES

Set of 7mm (UK 2/US 10 ½) DPNs

OTHER

Stitch marker

Cable needle

TENSION

11 sts and 15 rows over 10cm/4in over cable pattern worked in the round, using Kid Classic held double on 7mm (UK 2/US 10½) needles **before** felting.

SPECIAL ABBREVIATIONS

MB = Make bobble. K into the front, back, front, back & front of the next st to make 5 sts, turn, p5, turn, k5, turn, p2tog, p1, p2tog (3 sts), turn, k3tog (1 st).

C12F = Cable 12 sts to the front. Slip the next 6 sts onto the cable needle and hold at the front of the work, k the next 6 sts on the left-hand needle, then k the 6 sts from the cable needle.

SMITH SAYS

"See p 129 for further information about how to knit in the round on DPNs."

JAR HOLDER

Yarn is held DOUBLE throughout. With 7mm DPNs and yarn A, cast on 55 sts and arrange as evenly as possible between 3 needles. Taking care not to twist cast on edge, join to knit in the round and place stitch marker.

Purl 5 rnds.

Next rnd: Knit.

Purl 2 rnds.

Next rnd: *K4 with yarn A, MB with B, rep from * to end. (Note: you can carry yarn B along the WS of the work as you go rather than cutting yarn each time you MB).

Break off yarn B and cont in yarn A only.

Purl 2 rnds.

Main jar-holder section

Rnd 1: *P4, pfb, rep from * to end. 66 sts.

Rnd 2: Purl.

Rnd 3: *P5, pfb, rep from * to end. 77 sts.

Rnd 4: Purl.

Rnd 5: *P6, pfb, rep from * to end. 88 sts.

Rnd 6: (P43, pfb) twice. 90 sts.

Rnd 7: *P3, k12, rep from * to end.

Cable Section

Change to yarn B.

Rnd 1: *P3, C12F, rep from * to end.

Rnds 2 – 8: *P3, k12, rep from * end.

Rnds 1 – 8 form cable patt.

Cont in cable patt for a further 24 rnds.

Base Section

Change to yarn A.

Rnd 1: *P8, p2tog, rep from * to end. 81 sts.

Rnd 2: P1, *p8, p2tog, rep from * to end. 73 sts.

Rnd 3: Purl.

Rnd 4: *P8, p2tog, rep from * to last 3 sts, p3. 66 sts.

Rnd 5: *P4, p2tog, rep from * end. 55 sts.

Rnd 6: Purl.

Rnd 7: P1, *p2tog, rep from * to end. 28 sts.

Rnd 8: P2tog, rep from * to end.

Rnd 9: Purl.

Cut yarn leaving 20cm (8in) tail. Thread tail in a sewing up needle and pass yarn through the live sts, slipping them from the needles as you go. Draw to close and secure by sewing in end.

Turn bowl inside out. Fold the top brim down at the fold line (which will therefore now be the top rim of the bowl), and slip st in place, making sure not to pull the yarn too tight. Sew in all ends.

Wash at 60 degrees for approx 60 minutes (see notes). Once done and while still damp, pull the bowl into shape and fit over the container you want it to cover – I used a Kilner jar. Dry fully with the pot or jar in place.

FINISHED SIZE

Approx 38cm (15in) wide × 25cm (9¾in) high × 12cm (4¾in) deep after felting and excluding handles.

YARN

Rowan Felted TweedDK

50g (1¾oz)/ 175m (191yds) balls

A Cinnamon 175	7 × 50g
B Bilberry 151	1 × 50g
C Tawny 186	2 × 50g
D Mineral 181	1 × 50g
E Avocado 161	1 × 50g

NEEDLES

3.75mm (UK 9/US 5) circular needle, 100-120cm (40-47in) long

OTHER

Zip (zipper) – 45-50 cm (16-20in)
4 stitch markers
Strong sewing thread, to match A
Sewing needle
1 Pair bag handles (See Resources p 131)

SPECIAL ABBREVIATIONS

24 sts and 32 rows to 10cm/4in over st st on 3.75mm (UK 9/US 5) needles before felting.

JONES SAYS

"The bag is knitted then felted in the washing machine at 60 degrees using a 60 minute cycle. If your 60 degree cycle is longer, stop the washing after 50 minutes and then switch to brief rinse/spin cycle mode. Shorter than that is unlikely to felt the bag enough.

As washing machines can vary widely, knitting a 20cm (4in) square using yarn A and test washing it first before felting your bag is recommended.

The resulting felt should have no remaining stitch definition and should not fray when cut. If your felted bag is not thick, is not approximately the size given above after felting, and you can still see the knitted texture of the fabric, consider re-washing it at 40 degrees.

I use no fabric conditioner, just normal washing powder, tablets or liquid and a couple of Colour Catcher sheets.

Add a couple of old tea-towels or a non-shedding towel to the wash to add a bit of friction

Base of bag is worked in rows, and then bag is knitted in rounds until bag opening.

A rectangular base is knitted in rows before picking up and knitting stitches around the edges of base and then joining to work in the round from
that point.

If desired the pocket can be worked in a colour of your choice or in random stripes depending on how much yarn you have left after knitting the bag.

Stitch markers placed as per pattern indicate the 4 corners of the bag.

If a firmer base is desired, cut a piece of thick plastic or Pelmet Vilene slightly smaller than the base, cover with a layer of fabric or commercial felt and slip stitch into place at the corners to secure."

BAG

Using 3.75mm (US 5) needles and yarn A
cast on 122 sts.

Beg with a K row work 70 rows in st st,
ending with RS facing for next row.

Cast off until only 1 st remains and do not
break yarn.

With RS facing, turn work 90 degrees so
that you can begin picking up and knitting
along short edge of base, pick up 39 sts
(You will now have 40 sts including the st
left on needle after casting off). Place marker,
pick up and knit 122 sts along cast on edge
of base, place marker, then pick up and
knit 40 sts along second short edge, place
marker, then pick up and knit 122 sts along
cast off edge. 324 sts.

Place fourth marker and join to work in
rounds.

Beg with a K row, cont in st st, working
stripe sequence as follows:

Rnds 1 to 29: Yarn A.

Rnds 30 to 37: Yarn B.

Rnds 38 to 40: Yarn A.

Rnds 41 to 46: Yarn B.

Rnds 47 to 49: Yarn A.

Rnds 50 to 52: Yarn B.

Rnds 53 to 55: Yarn A.

Rnds 56 to 61: Yarn B.

Rnds 62 to 64: Yarn A.

Rnds 65 to 67: Yarn B.

Rnds 68 to 70: Yarn A.

Rnds 71 to 78: Yarn C.

Rnds 79 to 81: Yarn A.

Rnds 82 to 84: Yarn D.

Rnds 85 to 87: Yarn A.

Rnds 88 to 90: Yarn C.

Rnds 91 to 93: Yarn A.

Rnds 94 to 99: Yarn D.

Rnds 100 to 102: Yarn A.

Rnds 103 to 105: Yarn E.

Rnds 106 to 108: Yarn A.

Rnds 109 to 114: Yarn D.

Rnds 115 to 117: Yarn A.

Rnds 118 to 120: Yarn E.

Rnds 121 to 123: Yarn A.

Rnds 124 to 129: Yarn E.

Rnds 130 to 140: Yarn A.

BAG OPENINGS

Next rnd: Cont with Yarn A, cast off 40
sts between stitch markers, k122 and place
these st onto a stitch holder, cast off 40 sts, k
to end. 122 sts.

Side 1

With **WS** facing and beg with a P row work
17 rows in st st, ending with RS facing for
next row.

Next row (RS): Purl.

Rep last 18 rows twice, ending with **WS**
facing for next row.

Cast off knitwise.

With **WS** facing, rejoin yarn to rem 122 sts
and complete to match to Side 1.

MAKING UP

Tabs for handles & zip

Using 3.75mm (US 5) needles and Yarn A
cast on 58 sts.

Beg with a K row work in st st until work
measures 28cm (11in), ending with RS facing
for next row.

Cast off.

Pocket

Using 3.75mm (US 5) needles and Yarn C
cast on 82 sts.

Knit 2 rows.

Next row (RS): Knit.

Next row: K2, p to last 2 sts, k2.

These 2 rows set st st patt with garter st
border. Cont in patt until work measure
13cm (5in), ending with RS facing for next
row.

Knit 2 rows.

Cast off knitwise.

Weave in ends. Place the bag, square
for tabs, and the pocket in your washing
machine and wash at 60 degrees.

Once washed, remove from the machine
and firmly pull the bag into shape, especially
the corners of the sides. Pull the pockets
into shape. Stuff the bag with scrunched
up plastic bags, or a suitably sized plastic-
covered box to help hold the bag in shape
while it dries. If desired use clothes pegs or
similar at intervals down the sides, pinching
along the four corners of the bag to add

definition as it dries.

Place somewhere warm to dry, such as an
airing cupboard and leave to dry fully - this
may take a couple of days, then de-fluff the
felt inside and out if necessary.

Using strong sewing thread, slip stitch the
pocket inside the bag back, taking care to
only stitch part way through the felt of the
bag so it will not show on the outside.

Fold the openings down so the first garter
fold ridge you knitted is at the top edge of
the bag opening. Then fold it back on itself
again at the 2nd garter ridge and slip stitch
this garter ridge in place to inside of bag
along bag front/back (again taking care to
only stitch part way through the felt of the
bag), thus forming a hem to the top, with a
small flap on which to attach zip.

Cut 4 tabs 3 × 11cm (1¼ × 4¼in) or size
to suit your bag handles. Using photo as a
guide, sew the handles into place using
the tabs.

Stitch zip in place to bag opening flaps.

Cut a strip 3 × 8cm (1¼ × 3¼in), fold in half
around closed end of zipper end and stitch
in place to secure.

Pinch in the sides of the bag at top of each
corner by about 2.5cm (1 in) and secure
with a few stitches. Pull the stitches tightly so
that they 'bed in' to the felt and won't show
on the outside of the bag.

BIRCH GILET

FINISHED SIZE

	S	M	L	XL	XXL	
To fit Bust	81-86	91-97	102-107	112-117	122-127	cm
	32-34	36-38	40-42	44-46	48-50	in

YARN

Rowan Kid Classic 50g (1¾oz)/ 140m (153yds) balls

A Smoke 831	3	3	3	4	4	50g
B Pumice 888	4	4	5	5	6	50g

Rowan Kidsilk Haze 25g (1¾oz)/ 210m (230yds) balls

C Smoke 605	3	3	3	4	4	25g

NEEDLES

1 pair 4.5mm (UK 7/US 7) needles
1 pair 5mm (UK 6/US 8) needles
1 pair 6mm (UK4/US 10) needles

TENSION

25 sts and 26 rows over cable rib pattern
using yarn A on 5mm (UK 6/US 8) needles.
16 sts and 21 rows over st st using yarn
B and C held together on 6mm
(UK4/US 10) needles.

SPECIAL ABBREVIATIONS

C3F = slip next 2 sts onto cable needle
and leave at front, k1 tbl, slip 1 st back
from cable needle and purl this st, k1 tbl
remaining st from cable needle.
Tw2L = Knit into back of 2nd st on left
hand needle. Before taking this st off the
needle, knit into front of first st, then taking
both stitches off needle at same time.
Tw2R = Knit into 2nd st on left hand
needle. Before taking this st off the needle,
knit into first stitch, then take both sts off
needle at same time.

JONES SAYS

"The back is knitted vertically and
fronts are knitted horizontally.

For best results use the thumb
or a long tail cast-on as this
better complements the garter
stitch edging.

Working decreases 1 stitch in from
the edge at the armholes will give
a neater finish and make it easier
to pick up and knit from when
working the edgings."

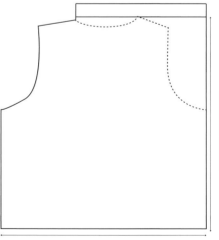

50.5 [54.5: 56.5: 58.5] cm

45.5 [51.5: 55.5: 61.5: 65.5] cm
(18 [20¼: 21¾: 24¼: 25¾] in)

BACK

Using yarn A and 5mm needles, cast on 114 [129: 139: 154: 164] sts.

Row 1 (RS): K1, *p2, k1 tbl, p1, k1tbl, rep from * to last 3 sts, p2, k1.

Row 2 (WS): K3, *p1 tbl, k1, p1 tbl, k2, rep from * to last st, k1.

Row 3: K1, *p2, C3F, rep from * to last 3 sts, p2, k1.

Row 4: As row 2.

These 4 rows set out cable rib pattern which is worked for back throughout.

Cont straight until work measures 29 [30: 31: 32: 33] cm (11½ [11¾: 12¼: 12½: 13} in), ending with RS facing for next row.

Shape armhole

Cast off 6 [8: 10: 13: 13] sts at beg of next 2 rows. 102 [113: 119: 128: 138] sts.

Dec 1 st at each end of next 5 [7: 9: 11: 11] rows, then foll 3 [4: 5: 5: 5] alt rows, then on 2 foll 4th rows. 82 [87: 87: 92: 102] sts.

Cont straight until armhole measures 20 [21: 22: 23: 24] cm (7¾ [8¼: 8¾: 9: 9½] in), ending with RS facing for next row.

Shape shoulders and back neck:

Cast off 7 [8: 8: 8: 9] sts at beg of next 2 rows. 68 [71: 71:76: 84] sts.

Next row (RS): Cast off 7 [8: 8: 8: 9] sts, pattern until there are 11[11: 11: 11: 12] sts on right needle and turn, leaving rem sts on a holder.

Work each side of neck separately.

Next row (WS): Cast off 4 sts, patt to end. Cast off rem 7 [7: 7: 7: 8] sts.

With RS facing, rejoin yarn to rem sts, cast off centre 32 [33: 33: 38: 42] sts, patt to end.

Complete to match first side, reversing shapings.

RIGHT FRONT

Using yarns B & C held together and 6mm (US 10) needles, cast on 97 [101: 103: 107: 109] sts.

Row 1 (RS): K1, p1, Tw2R, p3, k1 tbl, p1, k1 tbl, p3, Tw2L, p2, *k1, p1 rep from * to end.

Row 2 (WS): *P1, k1, rep from * to last 17 sts, k2, p2, k3, p1 tbl, k1, p1 tbl, k3, p2, k2.

Row 3: K1, p1, Tw2R, p3, C3F, p3, Tw2L, p2, *k1, p1 rep from * to end.

Row 4: As row 2.

Rows 5 and 6: As rows 1 and 2.

Row 7: K1, p1, Tw2R, p3, C3F, p3, Tw2L, p2, k to last 4 sts, (k1, p1) twice.

Row 8: (P1, k1) twice, p to last 17 sts, k2, p2, k3, p1 tbl, k1, p1 tbl, k3, p2, k2.

Row 9: K1, p1, Tw2R, p3, k1 tbl, p1, k1tbl, p3, Tw2L, p2, k to last 4 sts, (k1, p1) twice.

Row 10: As row 8.

Rows 7-10 set the patt of stocking st with cable panel to right edge and moss st border to left edge.

**Cont straight as set until work measures 31 [33: 35: 38: 41] cm 12¼ [13: 13¾: 15: 16¼] in), ending with RS facing for next row.

Divide for collar and shape shoulder

Next row (RS): Work 17 sts of cable pattern and place these on a st holder, cast on 1 st (for seam), work to end of row. 81 [83: 87: 91: 93] sts.

Work 7 [7: 7: 7: 9] rows, ending with RS facing for next row.

Dec 1 st at beginning of next and foll 8 [10:10:10:10]th row. 79 [81: 85: 89: 91] sts. Work 1 row, ending with RS facing for next row.

Shape armhole

Row 1: (RS): Cast off 22 [22: 21: 21: 22] sts at beg of next row. 57 [59: 64: 68: 69] sts.

Row 2 (WS): Work to last 3 sts, p2tog, k1. 56 [58: 63: 67: 68] sts.

Row 3: Cast off 3 sts, work to end. 53 [55: 60: 64: 65] sts.

Row 4: As row 2. 52 [54: 59: 63: 64] sts.

Row 5: Cast off 2 sts, work to end. 50 [52: 57: 61: 62] sts.

Row 6: As row 2. 49 [51: 56: 60: 61] sts.

Size XL and XXL only

Row 7: Cast off - [-: -: 2: 2] sts, work to end. 49 [51: 56: 58: 59] sts.

All sizes

Dec 1 st at armhole edge on next 0 [2: 4: 3: 3] rows, then on 2 [2: 2: 3: 3] foll alt rows, ending with RS facing for next row. 47 [49: 50: 52: 53] sts.

Work a further 5 [7: 9: 11: 11] rows, ending with **WS** facing for next row. Cast off in patt (NB: cast off edge forms right side seam).

LEFT FRONT

Using yarns B & C held together and 6mm (US 10) needles, cast on 97 [101: 103: 107: 109] sts.

Row 1 (RS): *P1, k1, rep from * to last 17 sts, p2, Tw2R, p3, k1 tbl, p1, k1tbl, p3, Tw2L, p1, k1.

Row 2 (WS): K2, p2, k3, p1 tbl, k1, p1 tbl, k3, p2, k2, *k1, p1, rep from * to end.

Row 3: *P1, k1, rep from * to last 17 sts, p2, Tw2R, p3, C3F, p3, Tw2L, p1, k1.

Row 4: As row 2.

Rows 5 and 6: As rows 1 and 2.

Row 7: (P1, k1) twice, k to last 17 sts, p2, Tw2R, p3, C3F, p3, Tw2L, p1, k1.

Row 8: K2, p2, k3, p1 tbl, k1, p1 tbl, k3, p2, k2, p to last 4 sts, (k1, p1) twice.

Row 9: (P1, k1) twice, k to last 17 sts, p2, Tw2R, p3, k1 tbl, p1, k1tbl, p3, Tw2L, p1, k1.

Row 10: As row 8.

Rows 7-10 set the patt of stocking st with cable panel to left edge and moss st border to right edge.

Complete as for right front from **, reversing all shapings.

MAKING UP

Sew in ends and press/block pieces. Join shoulders using back stitch or mattress stitch if preferred.

Armhole edgings

With RS facing, using Yarn A and 4.5mm (US 7) needles, pick up and knit 89 [96: 103: 111: 115] sts evenly all round armhole edge.

Knit 2 rows, ending with WS facing for next row.

Cast off knitwise.

Join side seams using back stitch, or mattress stitch if preferred.

Collar

Using Yarn B & C held together, with RS facing rejoin yarn to rem sts left on holder of right front. Cont in cable rib pattern until band, when slightly stretched, fits from shoulder to centre back neck, allowing an extra row for centre back seam.

Cast off in patt.

Rep for left front, then sew cast off edges of bands together to form centre back seam using back stitch or mattress stitch if preferred. Stitch neck band in place.

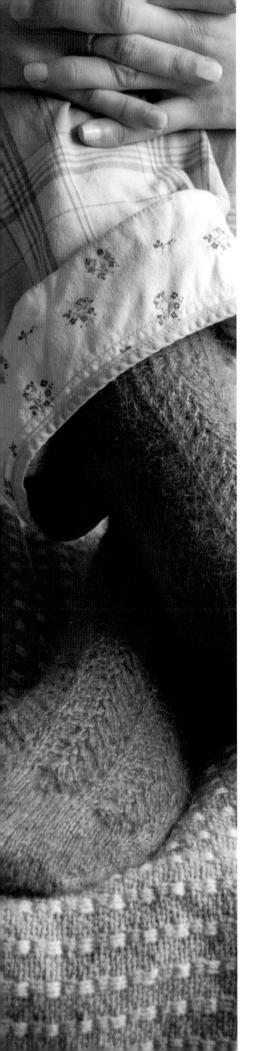

SNUG BED SOCKS

FINISHED SIZE
24cm (9½in) measured from back of heel to toe, laid out flat, unstretched.

YARN
Rowan Kidsilk Haze
25g (1oz)/210m (230yds) balls
A Majestic 589   2 x 25g
Rowan Fine Lace
50g (1¾oz)/400m (437yds) balls
B Vintage 926   1 x 50g

NEEDLES
2 x 3mm (UK size 11/US size US 2/3) fixed cable circular needles, 40 or 60cm (16 or 23-24 in) long

TENSION
32 sts and 40 rows to 10cm (4in) measured over st st on 3mm (UK 11/US 2/3) knitted with A & B held together, in the round on 2 circular needles.

SPECIAL ABBREVIATIONS
BN = bottom needle.
PU&K1 tbl = pick up a st and knit it through the back of the loop (see p 127)
PU&P1 = pick up and purl a st (see p 127)
TN = top needle

SMITH SAYS
"The socks are knitted from the toe up, using two short circular needles. This is a figure of eight cast on. See page 126 for our tutorial on this technique. The beauty of knitting socks this way is that you can try them on as you go.

When you work in rounds on 2 circular needles, you need to complete both needles to complete a round, the top needle (TN) or needle 1 AND the bottom needle (BN) or needle 2. I find it best to keep a track of this with numbers or a counter, and for the lace and also for the heel you may need to write down what you're doing and mark it off.

The lace happens only on the TN; the heel action takes place only on the BN.

This heel is a no-wrap version invented by Priscilla Wild.

The socks are stretchy and width-wise will fit most feet. To make them longer, try them on as you knit – assuming you add a few rounds and one or two lace pattern repeats, you will have enough yarn."

SOCKS (both alike)

Using 3mm (US size 2/3) needles, holding yarns A & B together, and using the figure of 8 toe-up cast on (see p 126 for this technique), cast on 14 sts onto each needle. TN will have 14 sts plus the slip knot that you started with. You have 28 sts altogether plus this slip knot which you will not work. Base round: TN: Knit all sts and this will feel and look oddly loose but don't worry, slip the starting slip knot but don't work it; BN: Knit all sts tbl.

Toe

Rnd 1: TN: K1, kfb, k to last 2 st (this will look like last 3 sts as the last of these is in fact the slip knot), kfb, k1, slip the slip knot off and pull it out gently to get rid of it; BN: As top needle except there is no slip knot. You have added 1 st on each of both needles. 32 sts (16 on each needle).

Rnd 2: Knit.

Rep rnds 1 & 2 until you have a total of 56 sts (28 on each needle) and ending with rnd 2.

Next rnd: TN: K1, kfb, k to last 2 sts, kfb, k1. 30 sts on TN; BN: Knit.

Next rnd: Both needles: Knit.

Next rnd: TN: K1, kfb, k to end. 31 sts; BN: Knit.

Next rnd: Both needles: Knit.

You now have 31 sts on the TN and 28 sts on the BN.

The lace patt will take place on the TN and the BN will be knitted.

Lace Patt

Rnd 1: TN: K2, *k1, yfwd, skpo, k2tog, k2, yfwd, k2, rep from * to last 2 sts, k2; BN: Knit.

Rnd 2: Both needles: Knit.

Rnd 3: TN: K2, *yfwd, k2, skpo, k2tog, k2, yfwd, k1, rep from * to last 2 sts, k2; BN: Knit.

Rnd 4: As rnd 2.

These 4 rnds set lace patt. Rep these 4 rnds a further 14 times, or until sock is length desired to heel placing (you can try it on for size), ending after rnd 4.

Place Heel

This will happen on BN only, and you will not work on the TN for a while. Whilst placing the heel you will work back and forth flat, working purl rows on the WS.

Next Row **(WS)**: Purl.

Shape Heel

Row 1: K27, turn.

Row 2: Sl 1, p25, turn.

Row 3: Sl 1, k24, turn.

Row 4: Sl 1, p23, turn.

Row 5: Sl 1, k22, turn.

Row 6: Sl 1, p21, turn.

Row 7: Sl 1, k20, turn.

Row 8: Sl 1, p19, turn.

Row 9: Sl 1, k18, turn.

Row 10: Sl 1, p17, turn.

Row 11: Sl 1, k16, turn.

Row 12: Sl 1, p15, turn.

Row 13: Sl 1, k14, turn.

Row 14: Sl 1, p13, turn.

Row 15: Sl 1, k12, turn.

Row 16: Sl 1, p11, turn.

You have systematically taken 8 sts 'out of play' on each end of this needle, 1 at a time as you worked ever-shorter rows. The sts you leave are the width of your heel-back.

Row 17: K10, k2tog, PU&K1 tbl, turn.

Row 18: Sl 1, p11, p2tog, PU&P1, turn.

Row 19: Sl 1, k12, k2tog, PU&K1 tbl, turn.

Row 20: Sl 1, k13, p2tog, PU&P1, turn.

Row 21: Sl 1, k14, k2tog, PU&K1 tbl, turn.

Row 22: Sl 1, p15, p2tog, PU&P1, turn.

Row 23: Sl 1, k16, k2tog, PU&K1 tbl, turn.

Row 24: Sl 1, p17, p2tog, PU&P1, turn.

Row 25: Sl 1, k18, k2tog, PU&K1 tbl, turn.

Row 26: Sl 1, p19, p2tog, PU&P1, turn.

Row 27: Sl 1, k20, k2tog, PU&K1 tbl, turn.

Row 28: Sl 1, p21, p2tog, PU&P1 turn.

Row 29: Sl 1, k22, k2tog, PU&K1 tbl, turn.

Row 30: Sl 1, p23, p2tog, PU&P1, turn.

Row 31: Sl 1, k24, k2tog, PU&K1 tbl, turn.

Row 32: Sl 1, p25, p2tog, PU&P1, turn.

Row 33: Sl 1, k27. 28 sts (now all back in play and the heel is turned).

Resume working in the round with TN worked in lace patt and BN worked as knit sts.

Work 12 of 4 row lace patt.

Next rnd: TN: K1, k2tog, k to end of needle. 30 sts; BN: Knit.

Next rnd: TN: K2, k2tog, k to last 4 sts, k2tog, k2. 28 sts; BN: Knit.

You now have 28 sts on each needle.

Cuff

Rnd 1: *K1 tbl, p1, rep from * to end.

This forms 1x1 twisted rib.

Cont in rib for 3cm (1¼in).

Cast-off: *Cast off 1 st, *(sl remaining st on RH needle back to LH needle, knit into this st and knit it off the needle) twice, k1, cast off 1 st, rep from * to end. (This forms a 2 st 'chain' between cast off sts).

MAKING UP

Sew in ends. No need to block but if you have a sock blocker, lightly spray socks, position on blocker and allow to dry.

LICHEN COWL

FINISHED SIZE

60cm (23½in) wide laid flat, or 120cm
(47¼in) circumference and 39.5cm
(15½in) deep.

YARN

Rowan Alpaca Colour
50g (1¾oz)/120m (131yds) skeins
Topaz 143   6 × 50g

NEEDLES

5.00mm (UK 6/US 8) circular needle,
100cm (40in) long

TENSION

18 sts and 28 rows to 10cm (4in) measured
over cobnut pattern worked in the round
on 5mm (UK 6/US 8) needles.

JONES SAYS

"For best results use the thumb or
a long tail cast-on as this better
complements the rib edging.

Place st marker at end of round
if desired.

When working the Cob nut pattern
the number of sts will inc to 324 on
rows 1 and 7, and dec back down
to 216 on rows 7 and 10."

COWL

Using 5.00mm (US 8) circular needle cast
on 216 sts.
Taking care not to twist cast on edge, work
in rounds as follows:
Rib rnd 1 (RS): *K2, p2, rep from * to end.
This sets 2 × 2 rib pattern. Work a further 7
rnds in rib.
Cob nut pattern
Rnd 1: *P3, (k1, yfwd, k1) into next st, rep
from * to end.
Rnd 2 and 3: *P3, k3; rep from * to end.
Rnd 4: *P3, k3tog, rep from * to end.
Rnd 5 and 6: Purl.
Rnd 7: *P1, (k1, yfwd, k1) into next st, p2,
rep from * to end.
Rnd 8 and 9: *P1, k3, p2, rep from * to
end.
Rnd 10: *P1, k3tog, p2, rep from * to end.
Rnd 11 and 12: Purl.
Rep rnds 1-12 a further 6 times, and then
work rnds 1-10 again.
Work 8 rnds in 2 × 2 rib as set out
previously.
Cast off in rib.

MAKING UP

Sew in ends. Lay Cowl out flat onto a level
surface, dampen with steam or spray with
water, gently pat into shape and leave to
dry thoroughly.

LICHEN MITTS

SIZE

To fit average female hand approximately
20cm (8in) circumference above thumb.
26cm (10in) long measured flat.

YARN

Rowan Alpaca Colour

50g (1¾oz)/120m (131yds) skeins

Topaz 143   2 x 50g

NEEDLES

1 pair 4.0mm (UK 8/US 6) needles
1 pair 4.5mm (UK7/US 7) needles
1 pair 5.00mm (UK 6/US 8) needles

TENSION

21 sts and 32 rows to 10cm/4in
measured over Cob nut pattern on
4mm (US 6) needles.

JONES SAYS

"Knitted flat, these simple mitts
are a breeze to knit, and are
shaped by simply decreasing the
size of needles used. If you prefer
to knit in the round, simply cast
on 2 sts fewer and work cob nut
pattern as for the Lichen Cowl.
When you come to divide for the
thumb, you don't need to work a
left or right thumb. Simply turn
and work 15 rows as per cob nut
pattern for mitts below, knitting
the st at thumb edge on every
row, and ending with WS facing
for next row. Then rejoin and
resume knitting in rounds to finish.

For best results use the thumb or
a long tail cast-on as this better
complements the rib edging.

If knitting the Lichen cowl also, you
will only need one additional skein
of yarn to make the mitts.

When working the Cob nut pattern
the number of sts will inc to 56 on
rows 1 and 7, and dec back down
to 38 on rows 7 and 10."

LEFT MITT

Using 5.00mm (US 8) needles cast on 38 sts.

Row 1 (RS): K2 *p2, k2, rep * to end.

Row 2: P2, *k2, p2, rep * to end.

This sets 2 x 2 rib pattern. Work a further 4 rows in rib, ending with RS facing for next row.

Cob nut pattern

Row 1 (RS): *P3, (k1, yfwd, k1) into next st, rep from * to last 2 sts, p2.

Row 2: K2, *p3, k3, rep from * to end.

Row 3: *P3, k3, rep from * to last 2 sts, p2.

Row 4: K2, *p3tog, k3, rep from * to end.

Row 5: Purl.

Row 6: Knit.

Row 7: *P1, (k1, yfwd, k1) into next st, p2, rep from * to last 2 sts, p2.

Row 8: K4, *p3, k3, rep from * to last 4 sts, p3, k1.

Row 9: *P1, k3, p2, rep from * to last 2 sts, p2.

Row 10: K4, *p3tog, k3, rep from * to last 4 sts, p3tog, k1.

Row 11: Purl.

Row 12: Knit.

Cont in patt as set, work a further 8 rows, ending with RS facing for next row.

Change to 4.5mm (US 7) needles and work 12 rows, ending with RS facing for next row.

Change to 4mm (US 6) needles and work a further 10 rows, ending with RS facing for next row.

Thumb opening

Keeping cob nut pattern correct throughout, cont as folls:

Next row (RS): Work 17 sts and turn, leaving 21 rem sts on a holder.

Work 14 rows on these 17 sts only for palm, knitting the st at thumb edge on every row and ending with WS facing for next row.

Break yarn and leave sts on a 2nd holder.

With RS facing, using 4mm (US 6) needles, rejoin yarn to sts on 1st holder and patt to end. 21 sts.

Work 14 rows on these 21 sts for back of hand, knitting the st at thumb edge on every row and ending with **WS** facing for next row.

Join sections

Next Row (WS): Work 21 sts of back hand in patt, then 17 sts of palm. 38 sts.

**Work a further 12 rows, ending with row 10 of cob nut pattern and with RS facing for next row.

Knit 3 rows.

Cast off knitwise.

RIGHT MITT

Work as given for left mitt to beg of thumb opening.

Thumb opening

Keeping cob nut pattern correct throughout, cont as folls:

Next Row (RS): Work 21 sts and turn, leaving 17 rem sts on a holder.

Work 14 rows on these 21 sts only for back of hand, knitting the st at thumb edge on every row and ending with **WS** facing for next row.

Break yarn and leave sts on a 2nd holder.

With RS facing, using 4mm (US 6) needles, rejoin yarn to sts on 1st holder and patt to end. 17 sts. Work 14 rows on these 17 sts for palm, knitting the st at thumb edge on every row and ending with **WS** facing for next row.

Join sections

Next Row (WS): Work 17 sts of palm in patt, then 21sts of back of hand. 38 sts. Complte as given for left mitt from **.

MAKING UP

Sew in ends. Lay mitts out flat onto a level surface, dampen with steam or spray with water, gently pat into shape and leave to dry thoroughly. Join side seams using mattress stitch or back stitch if preferred.

DAWN WRAP

FINISHED SIZE

47cm (18½in) × 162.5cm (64in).

YARN

Rowan Alpaca Colour

50g (1¾oz)/120m (131yds) skeins

Graphite 142   9 × 50g

NEEDLES

1 pair 4.5mm (UK 7/US 7) needles

Cable needle

OTHER

540 size 6 seed beads, approximately
4mm diameter (with hole large enough to
accommodate the yarn)

TENSION

25 st and 27 rows needles measured over
cable and bead pattern on 4.5mm (UK 7/US
7) needles.

SPECIAL ABBREVIATIONS

C3L = slip 2 sts to cable needle and hold
in front; k1 tbl; slip 2nd st on cable needle
back to left hand needle. P this st, then k1 tbl
from cable needle.

C4R = slip 2 sts to cable needle and hold in
back; k2; k2 from cable needle.

M1P = make 1 purlwise: Pick up loop
between last and next st from behind and
purl into the front of this loop.

PB = place bead: thread bead onto yarn
before starting. On RS row and with yarn
at front, bring bead close to needle, sl next
st purl wise and purl next st, leaving bead in
front of slipped st on RS of work.

T2L = sl 1 st to cable needle and hold in
front; p1; k1 tbl from cable needle.

T2R = sl 1 st to cable needle and hold in
back; k1 tbl; p1 from cable needle.

JONES SAYS

"See page 122 for more
information about knitting with
beads."

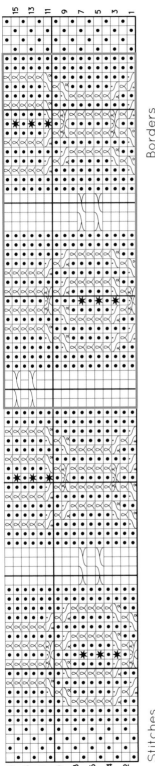

WRAP

Thread about 60 beads onto your ball of yarn before beginning the wrap (and onto each subsequent ball of yarn before you join in).

Using 4.5mm (US 7) needles cast on 108 sts.

Row 1: *K1, p1, rep from * to end.

Row 2: *P1, k1, rep from * to end.

These 2 rows set moss st. Work 3 rows more in moss stitch, ending with **WS** facing for next row.

Inc row (WS): (P1, k1) twice, *k4, (p1 tbl, k1) 4 times, k3, (p1, M1P) twice, k3, (p1 tbl, k2) twice, (p1, M1P) twice, rep from * once more, k4, (p1 tbl, k1) 4 times, k3, (p1, M1P) twice, (k2, p1 tbl) twice, k3, (p1 tbl, k2) twice, (p1, k1) twice. 118 sts.

Work rows 1-16 of cable and bead pattern as per chart or written instructions if preferred as follows:

Written instructions for 16 row pattern repeat

Row 1: (K1, p1) twice, *p2, (T2L, p1) twice, (T2R, p1) twice, p1, k4, p3, T2R, p1, C3L, p1, T2L, p3, k4, rep from * once more, p2, (T2L, p1) twice, (T2R, p1) twice, p1, k4, p3, T2R, p1, C3L, p1, T2L, p3, (k1, p1) twice.

Row 2: (P1, k1) twice, *k3, (p1 tbl, k2, p1 tbl, k1) twice, k2, p4, rep from * to last 19 sts, k3, (p1 tbl, k2, p1 tbl, k1) twice, k2, (p1, k1) twice.

Row 3: (K1, p1) twice, *p3, T2L, p1, C3L, p1, T2R, p3, k4, p2, T2R, p1, T2R, PB, (T2L, p1) twice, p1, k4, rep from * once more, p3, T2L, p1, C3L, p1, T2R, p3, k4, p2, T2R, p1, T2R, PB, (T2L, p1) twice, p1, (k1, p1) twice.

Row 4: (P1, k1) twice, *(k2, p1 tbl) twice, k3, (p1 tbl, k2) twice, p4, k4, (p1 tbl, k1) 4 times, k3, p4, rep from * once more, (k2, p1 tbl) twice, k3, (p1 tbl, k2) twice, p4, k4, (p1 tbl, k1) 4 times, k3, (p1, k1) twice.

Row 5: (K1, p1) twice, *p4, (k1 tbl, p1) 4 times, p3, C4R, (p2, k1 tbl) twice, p1, PB, p1, (k1 tbl, p2) twice, k4, rep from * once more, p4, (k1 tbl, p1) 4 times, p3, C4R, (p2, k1 tbl) twice, p1, PB, p1, (k1 tbl, p2) twice, (k1, p1) twice.

Rows 6 and 7: As rows 4 and 5.

Row 8: As row 4.

Row 9: (K1, p1) twice, *p3, T2R, p1, C3L, p1, T2L, p3, k4, p2, (T2L, p1) twice, (T2R, p1) twice, p1, k4, rep from * once more, p3, T2R, p1, C3L, p1, T2L, p3, k4, p2, (T2L, p1) twice, (T2R, p1) twice, p1, (k1, p1) twice.

Row 10: As row 2.

Row 11: (K1, p1) twice, *p2, T2R, p1, T2R, PB, (T2L, p1) twice, p1, k4, p3, T2L, p1, C3L, p1, T2R, p3, k4, rep from * once more, p2, T2R, p1, T2R, PB, (T2L, p1) twice, p1, k4, p3, T2L, p1, C3L, p1, T2R, p3, (k1, p1) twice.

Row 12: (P1, k1) twice, *k4, (p1 tbl, k1) 4 times, k3, p4, (k2, p1 tbl) twice, k3 (p1 tbl, k2) twice, p4, rep from * once more, k4, (p1 tbl, k1) 4 times, k3, p4, (k2, p1 tbl) twice, k3 (p1 tbl, k2) twice, (p1, k1) twice.

Row 13: (K1, p1) twice, *(p2, k1 tbl) twice, p1, PB, p1, (k1 tbl, p2) twice, k4, p4, (k1 tbl, p1) 4 times, p3, C4R, rep from * once more, (p2, k1 tbl) twice, p1, PB, p1, (k1 tbl, p2) twice, k4, p4, (k1 tbl, p1) 4 times, p3, (k1, p1) twice.

Rows 14 and 15: As rows 12 and 13.

Row 16: As row 12.

These 16 rows set out cable and bead pattern. Rep rows 1-16 a further 26 times until work measures approx 160cm (63in), then work rows 1-10 once more, ending with a RS facing for next row.

Next row (RS): (K1, p1) twice, *p2, T2R, p1, T2R, p1, (T2L, p1) twice, p1, k4, p3, T2L, p1, C3L, p1, T2R, p3, k4, rep from * once more, p2, T2R, p1, T2R, p1, (T2L, p1) twice, p1, k4, p3, T2L, p1, C3L, p1, T2R, p3, (k1, p1) twice.

Dec row (WS): P1, k1 twice, *k4, (p1 tbl, k1) 4 times, k3, (p2tog) twice, (k2, p1 tbl) twice, k3, (p1 tbl, k2) twice, (p2tog) twice, rep from * once more, k4, (p1 tbl, k1) 4 times, k3, (p2tog) twice, (k2, p1 tbl) twice, k3, (p1 tbl, k2) twice, (p1, k1) twice. 108 sts.

Work 5 rows in moss st as set previously, ending with a **WS** facing for next row.

Cast off loosely in moss st.

MAKING UP

Sew in ends & block lightly – I recommend pinning out flat (and without stretching). Spray with cool water using a plant spray, pat down and leave to dry fully. This will block your item gently without spoiling any of that lovely texture you have just created.

DUSK SCARF

FINISHED SIZE

26cm (10¼in) x 162cm (63¾in)

YARN

Rowan Fine Art

100g (3½oz)/400m (437yds) skeins

Raven 304   2 x 100g

NEEDLES

1 pair 3mm (UK 11/US 2-3) needles

Cable needle

TENSION

34 sts and 34 rows over cable and rib
pattern on 3mm (UK 11/US 2-3) needles

SPECIAL ABBREVIATIONS

C4B = slip 2 sts to cable needle and hold at
back of work; k2; k2 from cable needle.

MIP = make 1 purlwise: Pick up loop
between last and next st from behind and
purl into the front of this loop.

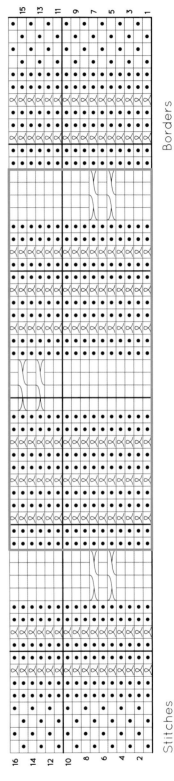

SCARF

Using 3mm/UK 11/US 2 or 3 needles, cast on 78 sts.

Row 1 (RS): *K1, p1, rep from * to end.

Row 2 (WS): *P1, k1, rep from * to end.

These 2 rows set moss stitch pattern. Cont in moss st for 3 rows, ending with **WS** facing for next row.

Inc row (WS): (P1, k1) twice, k2, (p1 tbl, k2) twice, *(p1, M1P) twice, (k2, p1 tbl) 3 times, k2, rep from * to last 14 sts, (p1, M1P) twice, (k2, p1 tbl) twice, k2, (p1, k1) twice. 88 sts.

Cable and rib pattern

Work rows 1-16 of cable and rib pattern as per chart or written instructions if preferred as follows:

Written instructions for cable and rib pattern

Row 1 (RS): (K1, p1) twice, *(p2, k1 tbl) twice, p2, k4, p2, k1 tbl) rep from * to last 9 sts, p2, k1 tbl, p2, (k1, p1) twice.

Row 2: (P1, k1) twice, *(k2, p1 tbl) twice, k2, p4, k2, p1 tbl, rep from * to last 9 sts, k2, p1 tbl, k2, (p1, k1) twice.

Rows 3-4: As rows 1 and 2.

Row 5: (K1, p1) twice, (p2, k1 tbl) twice, p2, *C4B, (p2, k1 tbl) 3 times, p2, k4, (p2, k1 tbl) 3 times, p2, rep from * to last 16 sts, C4B, (p2, k1 tbl) twice, p2, (k1, p1) twice.

Row 6: (P1, k1) twice, *(k2, p1 tbl) twice, k2, p4, k2, p1 tbl, rep from * to last 9 sts, k2, p1 tbl, k2, (p1, k1) twice.

Rows 7-8: As rows 5 and 6.

Row 9-12: As rows 1 and 2.

Row 13: (K1, p1) twice, (p2, k1 tbl) twice, p2, *k4, (p2, k1 tbl) 3 times, p2, C4B, (p2, k1 tbl) 3 times, p2, rep from * to last 16 sts, k4, (p2, k1 tbl) twice, p2, (k1, p1) twice.

Row 14: (P1, k1) twice, *(k2, p1 tbl) twice, k2, p4, k2, p1 tbl, rep from * to last 9 sts, k2, p1 tbl, k2, (p1, k1) twice.

Rows 15-16: As rows 13 and 14.

These 16 rows set cable and rib pattern. Rep these 16 rows 32 times, then work rows 1-11 of patt once more, ending with **WS** facing for next row.

Dec row (WS): (P1, k1) twice, k2, (p1 tbl, k2) twice, *p2tog twice, (k2, p1 tbl) 3 times, k2, rep from * to last 16 sts, p2tog twice, (k2, p1 tbl) twice, k2, (p1, k1) twice. 78 sts.

Work 5 rows in moss stitch pattern, ending with **WS** facing for next row.

Cast off in patt loosely.

MAKING UP

Sew in ends & block lightly – I recommend pinning out flat (and without stretching). Spray with cool water using a plant spray, pat down and leave to dry fully. This will block your item gently without spoiling any of that lovely texture you have just created.

USEFUL INFORMATION

GENERAL

Instructions are given for the smallest size and, where relevant, alternative measurements and/or instructions relating to larger sizes are in square brackets - [ ]. Where only one figure or instruction is given, this applies to all sizes. Where a ' - ' or '0' is given for the size you are knitting, then that specific instruction does not apply to your particular size.

Instructions that are enclosed in round brackets - ( ) are to be worked the number of times stated, e.g. (k1, p1) twice = k1, p1, k1, p1.

TENSION

The quantities of yarn specified for each design are approximate and based on average requirements for the tension stated. To achieve the size and fit intended it is essential that you match the tension stated, and we recommend you swatch for tension before knitting the project.

Swatching for tension

Tension is conventionally expressed as the number of stitches and rows that make up a 10cm (4in) square in the stitch pattern stated. However, knitting only a 10cm (4in) square will be too scant for taking an accurate measure of the tension/gauge. Stitches along the edges will always be a little tighter than the rest, so you will need to make a swatch that is larger than this. It may be helpful to work a garter stitch border around your swatch area to enable the edges to lay flatter, thus aiding measurement. We recommend multiplying the number of stitches and rows by approximately 1½ to give you an adequately sized swatch. You may wish to round this up or down if desired for convenience. For example if you are working a patterned swatch you will want to have a number that works with the pattern repeat, plus stitches for a garter stitch border if you intend to include one.

Adjusting needle size

If you have too few stitches to those required this means your tension is looser than required and you need to choose a smaller needle size to tighten it. Likewise, if you have too many stitches your tension is tighter than required and you need to choose a larger needle size. If you are only 1-2 stitches out, try adjusting by 1 needle size up/down, if you are more than 2 out, try 2 sizes up/down - then you need to make another swatch with the new needles.

CHARTS

Using charts in knitting has many benefits and some types of knitting, particularly lace and colourwork, are best expressed in this format. Many knitters struggle with reading charts, yet it is so easy to do once you know how. We hope the following tips will clarify and make this process easier.

Reading charts

A chart is used to visually represent your knitting as if you were looking at it from the front, and so right side rows are read from right to left, whereas wrong side rows are read from left to right. However, when an item is knitted in the round, each line of the chart is read from right to left as all the rounds are knitted on the right side.

Each square represents a stitch or stitch manoeuvre, and different stitches are indicated with symbols which are explained in a key (sometimes called a legend). One thing knitters can find confusing is that although a stitch manoeuvre may require more than one stitch, such as k2tog, this is represented as a single square on a chart. However, these extra stitches taken will be accounted for at some point further along the row either with an increase, a 'no stitch' or shaping. The trick is not to over-think it, just work along square by square doing whatever the symbols are dictating.

Useful tips

• photocopy the chart you are working from (in colour if relevant) and enlarge it so that it is easier to read, this has an added benefit as you can cross off each row worked with pen/pencil without spoiling your main copy
• read the chart carefully before starting your work and familiarise yourself with the stitches listed in the key
• when working intarsia, read a row ahead so that you can carry yarns to the correct position ready for the next row
• use Post-It notes to mark your place and then move them up row by row as you progress

FINISHING

After investing so much time in knitting your item you will want to reward your efforts by having it look the best it can. A professional finish can be achieved with the following tips.

Darning in ends

This can be done before or after blocking according to your personal preference. Darn ends in neatly along a seam edge where possible and take care to darn along areas of the same colour where this is relevant.

Pressing and blocking

This is essential for achieving a good finish and no sewing up should start until this stage has been done. Always pin out your work to the correct measurements stated in the pattern, and press in accordance with the ball band suggestions using an ironing cloth to protect it. Always press lightly with a straight up and down action rather than with circular movements, and never press rib or moss stitch at all. Alternatively, for textured stitches and delicate yarns simply mist with clean water using a plant spray, patting lightly to ensure the water goes into the fibres (or lay a damp white cotton cloth over it). Let the work dry out completely before you unpin it.

Sewing up

When sewing pieces together, take care to ensure that any areas of texture or colour line up accurately where they join. Use a stitch such as mattress stitch or backstitch for all seams unless otherwise stated. Once completed, gently press any seams or hems.

Washing instructions – see ball band.

EXPERIENCE RATING

As perceptions of ease or difficulty will vary for individual knitters, this is for guidance only. All our patterns have been rated in terms of level of ease to knit and this is indicated using the following symbols:

Easy, straightforward knitting suitable for new knitters or more experienced who want an easy knit.

Includes intermediate techniques - suitable for knitters with moderate experience.

Includes more advanced techniques - suitable for more experienced knitters or those that like a challenge.

GENERAL ABBREVIATIONS

Special abbreviations are included within the relevant patterns.

alt	alternate
approx	approximately
beg	beginning; begin; begins
cont	continue
cm	centimetre(s)
dec	decreas(e)(ing)
DPN(s)	double pointed needles(s)
foll	following; follow
inc	increase(e)(ing)
in(s)	inch(es)
k	knit
k2tog	knit the next 2 stitches together
k3tog	knit the next 3 stitches together
kfb	knit into front and back of same stitch
LH	left hand
mm	millimetre(s)
p	purl

patt	pattern
p2tog	purl the next 2 stitches together
p3tog	purl the next 3 stitches together
pfb	purl into front and back of same stitch
rem	remain(ing)
rep	repeat
rev st st	reverse stocking stitch
rnd(s)	round(s)
RH	right hand
RS	right side
skpo	slip 1, knit 1, pass slipped stitch over
sl	slip
st(s)	stitch(es)
st st	stocking stitch (i.e. knit all RS rows, purl all WS rows)
tbl	through back loop
WS	wrong side
yb	yarn back
yfrn	yarn forward round needle (an increase): bring the yarn to the front, then all the way around the needle again – the extra stitch – the yarn will then be in position to purl the next stitch
yfwd	bring yarn to front of work before knitting the next stitch.
yrn	yarn round needle (an increase): take yarn from the front over the needle to the back ready to knit the next stitch thus making an extra stitch

USA GLOSSARY

Cast off = bind off

Moss stitch = seed stitch

Tension = gauge

Stocking stitch = stockinette stitch

Yarn forward, yarn round needle, or yarn forward round needle = yarn over

TECHNIQUES

This section includes tutorials on how to work some of the more advanced techniques used in the designs and includes:

How to knit 'toe-up' socks on 2 circular needles

Knitting pleats

Knitting Fairisle in the round

Knitting intarsia

Knitting with double pointed needles

Knitting with beads

Other useful information and general abbreviations can be found on page 118-119

KNITTING WITH BEADS

Adding beads is a great way to embellish knitting and is surprisingly easy to do. Choose beads that are washable and colourfast, with a hole wide enough to accommodate the yarn. As a guide, size 6 beads work well with double knitting weight yarns, and size 8 are suitable for 4ply and finer yarns.

The method we have used is slip stitch beading. Beads are threaded onto the yarn before knitting, and using a small piece of felt when doing so will help stop the beads from rolling onto the floor. We recommend threading no more than 200 beads at a time, breaking the yarn to thread more if needed before rejoining. This minimises wear on the yarn when sliding beads along it, and excess beads can make for uncomfortable knitting, affecting tension as a result.

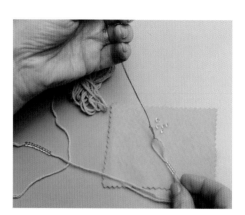

Threading up the beads

With a sewing needle fine enough to pass through the beads, thread with approx 15 cm (6in) of cotton sewing thread and tie the ends together to make a loop. Hang the 'tail' of your yarn through this loop. Pick up beads and slide them down the needle and thread onto the yarn.

Placing beads when knitting on a right side row

1 Knit to where the bead needs to be placed, slide a bead up yarn close to your work, and bring the yarn forward (as if to purl).

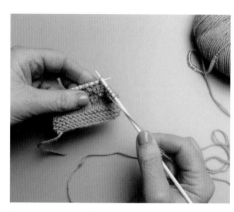

2 Slip the next stitch purlwise.

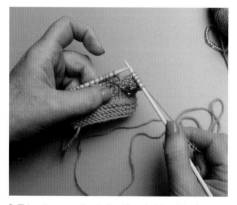

3 Take the yarn back (as if to knit), with the bead placed on the right side on top of the slipped stitch.

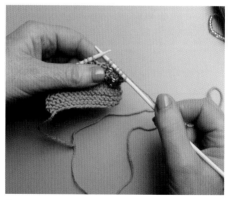

4 Knit the following stitch firmly, trapping the bead in place. On the following row, gently push bead to the right side if it has slipped to the back before working the slipped stitch firmly.

Placing beads when purling on a right side row

1 Worked in a similar way to above, although the beads will be less securely anchored than when placing on a knit row. Purl to where the bead needs to be placed and, keeping the yarn forward, slide a bead up close to your work.

2 Slip the next stitch purlwise.

Placing beads when purling on a wrong side row

1 Purl to where the bead needs to be placed, slide a bead up yarn close to your work and take the yarn to the back (as if to knit).

2 Slip the next stitch purlwise.

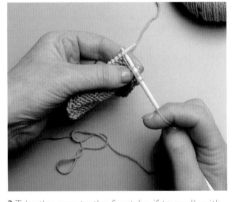

3 Take the yarn to the front (as if to purl), with the bead placed on the right side on top of the slipped stitch.

4 Purl the following stitch firmly, securing the bead in place on the right side. On the following row, reposition bead if needed before working the slipped stitch firmly.

SHIBORI KNITTED FELT

Originating from an ancient Japanese craft, shibori refers to the process of introducing resistant elements by twisting, tying or pinching in areas of fabric to prevent treatments from penetrating into those areas. Perhaps more commonly associated with tie-dyeing fabrics, these principles can also be applied to create exciting textural effects to knitted wool which is then felted. For example, 'bumps' can be formed by tying in marbles before felting, as the knitting stretched around the marble cannot move and therefore cannot felt like other areas of the knitting.

Once the marble is removed, its shape remains with the stitches clearly visible on the 'bumps'. Many surface embellishments can be achieved using shibori techniques, and another we have shared below is weaving in silk strands. Silk fibres are resistant to felting, but by weaving them into the knitting before felting the fibres are gathered in and trapped within the felt, adding colour and textural interest.

Tying in marbles to make 'bumps'
You will need marbles and lengths of non-woollen thread. Mark where you would like the marbles to be with a short length of thread pulled through the knitting as, once a marble is tied into the work, the knitting becomes distorted and it is difficult to judge accurate placement of the remaining marbles.

1 With the marble held on the wrong side, positon the marble at the point you have marked and stretch the fabric tightly over it. The marble works as a resist and the knitting that is tied around it will felt very little, so make sure it is not over-stretched.

2 Using a non-felting thread, such as 4 ply cotton yarn, tie the thread really firmly, going round the 'neck' of the marble twice and double-knotting the thread. Cut the ends to approximately 3cm (1in) in length.

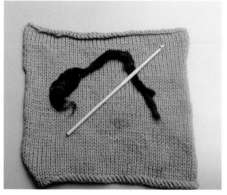

Weaving in silk strands
You will need some pieces of silk fibres and a crochet hook. Cut or tear the pieces of silk to lengths as desired. On the Shibori Bowl, I used pieces that were 7-10cm (2¾ -4in) long.

1 With the silk held on the right side, and using the crochet hook, pull the silk through the work.

2 Pull the silk through the work again a little further along, leaving 'bumps' in the middle, and 'tails' that will be loose after felting. Do not worry if it feels a little loose at this stage; once the work is felted, the silk will be firmly trapped into the surface of the knitting.

INTARSIA

Intarsia is the method used to create separate areas of colour as you knit. It is usually worked in stocking stitch, using separate lengths of yarn for each section of colour to create a single layer fabric. This is different from the Fairisle technique where yarns are carried across the back of the work. Most intarsia designs are worked according to a chart, joining in and fastening off colours as needed. It is not usually practical to work with whole balls of yarn and so you should wind the necessary amount onto a bobbin. You can make your own, but for ease of use and convenience we recommend using plastic knitting bobbins.

For very large areas of a single colour you may prefer to use a separate ball rather than a bobbin, but to avoid this becoming unravelled and tangled, wrap the ball in a small plastic bag secured with a rubber band. Before starting you will need to read through your pattern to assess how many bobbins will be needed for each individual block of colour.

When joining in or breaking off yarns it is best to leave tails which are at least 12cm (4¾in) long so you have enough to sew in with. Ends need to be neatly darned/sewn into place at the back of the work. Carefully darn the ends in along shapes of the same colour.

Winding bobbins

First wind bobbins of the yarn colours you are using. Unless only a very small amount of one colour is needed it is helpful to wind as much yarn as you can fit onto the bobbin. That way you will not run out too frequently, and avoid having too many ends to sew in afterwards.

'Locking' bobbins

An advantage of using plastic bobbins is that the end of the yarn can be wrapped around the tip of the bobbin to secure and prevent it unravelling when not in use when you are knitting.

Joining in a new colour

1 Work in the first colour until you reach the stitch before the one where you want the new colour to start. Insert the right needle into the next stitch. Place the new colour over the right hand needle with the tail to the back and work the next stitch with the existing colour.

2 Move the existing yarn and the new tail end over to the left and drop, bringing the new yarn up from underneath and begin knitting with the new colour.

Changing colours

When changing colour across a row, it is essential that the yarns are crossed over at the back of the work to prevent holes forming . Cross the yarns by taking the existing yarn over to the left and drop, bringing the new yarn up from underneath and knit the next stitch firmly with the new colour.

TOE UP SOCKS

Starting with a figure of 8 cast on provides a seamless toe, and enables you to try the sock on for size as it is knitted. When knitting socks with 2 circular needles you will work half of the stitches always on one needle, with the remaining stitches always on a second needle. Instead of turning your work as you do in a flat piece, you will rotate the work clockwise with the front always facing you. Knitting the stitches off the first needle, then rotating and knitting the stitches on the second needle will result in having knitted a full round.

The neat heel shaping can be achieved by picking up stitches from the work two rows down and knitting through the back loop. We have included how to do this on both knit and purl rows.

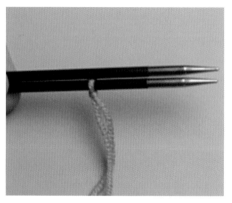

1 Figure of 8 cast on
Make a slip knot and place this onto the first of the needles. This slip knot is only to anchor the yarn as you cast on and will not count as a stitch. Hold the second needle above the first ready to begin casting on to both needles at the same time.

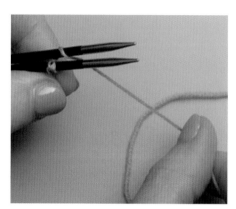

2 Beginning with the working yarn held at the back, use a figure of eight movement to wrap the working yarn around the needles thus: bring it up and over the top needle to the front, then between the needles again to the back, then down and under the bottom needle round to the front , then between the needles again to the back. You will now have a stitch on each needle (do not count the slip stitch).

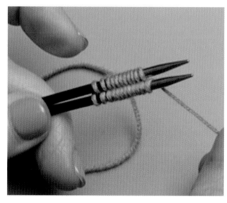

3 Continue wrapping with this figure of eight motion until you have the required number of stitches on each needle (which will be the same number per needle plus the slip knot), ending with the yarn at the back.

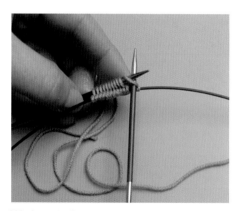

Working the first rounds
4 Pull the bottom needle to the right so its stitches are suspended on the cable of that needle and let it hang free. Then knit across the stitches on the top needle using the other tip of the same circular needle.

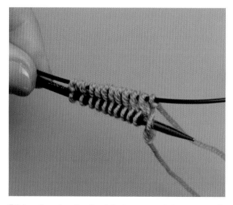

5 Now keeping the front facing you, rotate your work clockwise so that the stitches you have just knitted are on the bottom.

6 Slide the stitches you've just worked on to the flexible able part of the needle & let it hang free. Slide the needle on top so its stitches are on the tip ready to work, slip the slip knot but do not work it, then knit across these stitches THROUGH THE BACK LOOPS using the other tip of the same circular needle. You will now have completed one full round. This is the only time you will need to knit into the back loops, and all other rounds are worked in the usual way.

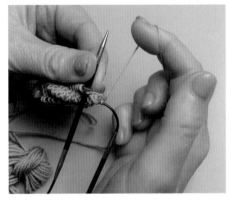

7 Rotate the work clockwise as before and knit across the stitches on the top needle as before. Rotate the work clockwise again, drop the slip knot and pull it out before knitting across the stitches on that needle and completing this second full round.

8 The toe of your sock will look like this.

To eliminate the 'ladder' between needles:
You can do this by firmly pulling the yarn upwards for both the first and second stitches of each new needle.

PU&K1 tbl - Pick up and knit a stitch through the back of the loop
1 With the tip of the left-hand needle, pick up the front leg of the stitch 2 rows below.

2 Knit into this 'stitch' through the back of the loop.

PU&P1 – Pick up and purl a stitch
With the tip of the left-hand needle, pick up the purl 'bump' of the stitch 2 rows below and purl it.

KNITTED PLEAT

Pleats can be created by making the knitting wider than would normally be required, and then folding the knitted fabric back on itself first in one direction to make the return, and then in the in the opposite direction to make the front. Pleats are 'Z' shaped and consist of a front, return and back which all need to have the same amount of stitches, so you will need to cast on three times the number of stitches of the desired pleat width. As the pleat consists of 3 layers, finer yarns are recommended to avoid bulk.

Permanent folds can be created by slipping the stitches where the fold lines are required. Using stitch markers can be helpful to remind you where these are placed along the row. The fold will sit in a different direction depending on whether the working yarn is placed at the back or front of the work when slipping these stitches. On RS rows slipping the stitch with the yarn at the back on a RS row will result in a fold that goes from right to left, whereas slipping with the yarn at the back will result in a fold that goes from left to right.

Once you have completed your knitting with fold lines you will need to fold and knit in your pleat using 2 double pointed needles (DPNs).

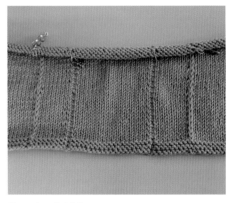

Creating fold lines
Fold lines created to form an inverted box pleat as described above

Folding pleats
1 Work to the start of the pleat front. Slip the pleat front stitches (including the fold line stitch) onto a DPN, then slip the stitches of the return (including the fold line stitch) onto your second DPN. There needs to be the same number of stitches on each needle.

2. Turn the second DPN 180 degrees so the return stitches are parallel with the front stitches with their wrong sides facing each other.

3 Position the 2 DPNs in front of the remaining stitches on left hand needle ready to knit the layers together.

4 Begin knitting together one stitch from each of the three needles. Repeat until you have worked your way across all stitches on the DPNs.

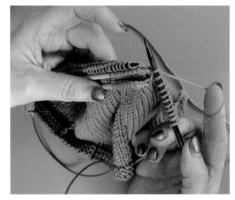

5 Repeat steps 1-4 for the other side of the inverted box pleat, reversing the direction of folding. Work to the end of the row to complete.

DOUBLE POINTED NEEDLES

Double Pointed Needles (DPNs) are usually available in sets of four or five and are used for knitting in the round. Long DPNs can be used for larger work, but it is more common to use shorter needles for making tubes of knitting that are too small to comfortably knit with a circular needle, such as with cuffs and neck bands.

Getting started
Cast the stitches onto one DPN.

2 Distribute the stitches as evenly as possible onto 3 DPNs and check that the stitches are not twisted. Place the stitch marker, which is used to denote the beginning of each new round of knitting.

3 With only 3 of the DPNs in use (the 4th will be used shortly), work the first stitch. This joins the knitting into the round and traps the stitch marker between 2 stitches.

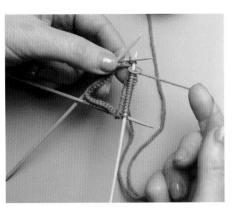

4 Using the needle now freed up, move round to the set of stitches on the next DPN and work these. Once you have done this 3 times, and knitted the stitches on the last needle, you will reach the stitch marker. Slip the marker from the left to the right needle and continue onto Round 2.

5 To help prevent the slight 'ladder' that can occur between the needles, you can move the stitches along by two to three every few rounds. To do this, when you reach the end of the stitches on one DPN, work an additional two or three stitches from the next needle before re-introducing the 4th DPN.

6 You can also help to reduce the ladder by firmly pulling the working yarn up-wards as you work the 2nd stitch on each new DPN.

KNITTING FAIRISLE IN THE ROUND

Fairisle is a traditional Scottish method of working with two colours across a row to make patterns consisting of small motifs. Colours not being worked are stranded loosely across the back of your knitting, forming 'floats' or 'strands' which create a double thickness of fabric. It is best not to strand over more than three consecutive stitches, and where this is required you will need to catch in the non working yarn every two or three stitches by 'weaving' or 'carrying' it.

When stranding or carrying yarns it is essential not to pull the yarns too tight to maintain correct tension and elasticity in the work.

Fairisle can be worked flat in rows, but traditionally it was worked in the round. It is quicker and easier to strand when working knit stitches, and working in the round eliminates the purl rows when working stocking stitch. Stitches can be stranded by either the one-handed or two-handed method.

Fairisle: One-handed

The yarn not in use is carried across the back of the work, forming strands or floats. To make sure that these are lying parallel to each other, and are not twisted decide at the outset which yarn is going to be on top, and which is going to be underneath. Begin by knitting in the first shade to the point where the second shade is to be used. Drop or hold the first strand away and pick up and knit with the second strand. Knit the number of stitches indicated with the second strand, and then pick up the first strand again. Note how the blue yarn is coming from below the white yarn.

Fairisle: Two-handed

1 Hold the new colour over the left forefinger, and the first colour over your right.

2 Pick up the yarn that is in your left hand (in these pictures this is the blue yarn) by placing your needle over the yarn and scooping it up.

3 Continue along the row, knitting the first colour with your right hand, and picking up the new colour from your left as in step 2.

4 Change yarns consistently each time to ensure the floats are as flat and as horizontal as possible. In this illustration, the pale yarn is always 'on top' of the dark yarn and the floats are fairly relaxed but not baggy.

RESOURCES

ROWAN YARNS
www.knitrowan.com

www.westminsterfibers.com

BEADS
Debbie Abrahams Beads

www.debbieabrahamsbeads.co.uk

SILKS
You can use Solo or Spectrum silk fibres (for weaving into the felted bowls). www.texere-yarns.co.uk

MARBLES
You need bog-standard small marbles (for the Shibori bowl), 14–17mm (1–1½in). Available from most toy and discount shops or from The House of Marbles. www.houseofmarbles.com

CLOAK FASTENER
Celtic Elven Pewter Clasps (for Boreal Capelet) by ModelfikAccessories on Etsy. www.etsy.com/uk/shop/ ModelfikAccessories

BUTTONS
Ceramic Heart Snowflake Buttons (for the Landscape cushion), 3.5cm (1¾in) diameter by TerracottaToys on Etsy. www.etsy.com/shop/TerracottaToys

Slate buttons (for the Coastal cushion), size medium by DriftNiceties on Etsy. www.etsy.com/uk/shop/DriftNiceties

Shell buttons (for Cockleshell cardigan), 14mm (½in) diameter from John Lewis.

BAG HANDLES
Branches laser cut handles (for Bramble Stripe bag) by Lumie Designs. www.lumiedesign.com

SMITH & JONES KNITS WEBSITE
For all the latest updates, blog and information about the designs. www.smithandjonesknits.com

ACKNOWLEDGEMENTS

Smith & Jones would like express their sincere gratitude to the following, without whom this book would not have been created:

Rowan for the beautiful yarns, and David and Kate for their support throughout.

Sarah Hatton for her expert technical advice & support.

Graphic designer, Emma Chapman, for bringing our ideas to life so beautifully.

Will Reed for additional photography support.

Our wonderful models:
Caroline Chapman, Lily Crowther-Smith, Eithwen Morgan and Kevin Lawlor.

We are also grateful to Neath Port Talbot County Borough Council for allowing us to use the glorious Margam Park as one of our locations.

INDIVIDUAL THANKS
Smith would like to thank her amazing knitters, Kath Morgan, Hilda Farley, Jean Marshall and Celia Wood. I actually love you. Her thanks also to Thi, manicurist to the Kniteratti.

Jones thanks her long suffering husband Dave who encourages her in all she does; Jane & Gary Chilvers and Lynne & Rob Taylerson whose support and unfailing cheerleading have eased the journey; and her fantastic knitters: Fiona Winning, Anne Haddrill and Dany Dalley.

GALLERY

Drift Folded Shrug

Alison Crowther-Smith

Main image pages **8**

Pattern page **60-61**

Ice Boa in Cocoon

Alison Crowther-Smith

Main image pages **10**

Pattern page **62-63**

Rime Fairisle Snood

Alison Crowther-Smith

Main image pages **12**

Pattern page **64-65**

Ice Boa

Alison Crowther-Smith

Main image pages **14**

Pattern page **66-67**

Landscape Cushion

Alison Crowther-Smith

Main image pages **24, 25**

Pattern page **76-77**

Kitchen Garden Tunic

Donna Jones

Main image pages **26**

Pattern page **78-80**

Garden Song Blanket

Donna Jones

Main image pages **28, 29**

Pattern page **81-86**

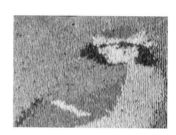

Garden Song Cushion

Donna Jones

Main image pages **31**

Pattern page **87-88**

Boreal Capelet

Alison Crowther-Smith

Main image pages **40, 41**

Pattern page **98-99**

Nest Felted Containers

Alison Crowther-Smith

Main image pages **42**

Pattern page **100-104**

Stripe Bramble Bag

Donna Jones

Main image pages **45**

Pattern page **104-105**

Birch Gilet

Donna Jones

Main image pages **46**

Pattern page **106-107**

Ice Cuffs

Alison Crowther-Smith

Main image pages **16, 17**

Pattern page **68-69**

Drifted Folded Cuff Mitts

Alison Crowther-Smith

Main image pages **18,19**

Pattern page **70-71**

Rise Scarf

Alison Crowther-Smith

Main image pages **20**

Pattern page **72-73**

Landscape Throw

Alison Crowther-Smith

Main image pages **23**

Pattern page **74-75**

Lumi Mittens

Alison Crowther-Smith

Main image pages **32, 33**

Pattern page **89**

Cockleshell Cardigan

Donna Jones

Main image pages **35**

Pattern page **91-93**

Coastal Bed Runner

Donna Jones

Main image pages **36, 37**

Pattern page **94-95**

Coastal Cushion

Donna Jones

Main image pages **38**

Pattern page **96-97**

Snug Bed Socks

Alison Crowther-Smith

Main image pages **48, 49**

Pattern page **108-109**

Lichen Cowl & Mitts

Donna Jones

Main image pages **50, 53**

Pattern page **110-112**

Dawn Wrap

Donna Jones

Main image pages **54, 55**

Pattern page **113-114**

Dusk Scarf

Donna Jones

Main image pages **56**

Pattern page **115-116**

ABOUT THE AUTHORS

Alison and Donna, who are Smith & Jones, are united by their artistic differences. Their individual approaches to their craft create a vibrant and highly complementary collection, achieving a sense of design balance that can elude a solo-designer.

Smith & Jones invite you to visit them at www.smithandjonesknits.com where, as well as keeping up to date with all their latest news, you can access on-line support and information about the designs.

SMITH

Alison Crowther-Smith has been knitting for many years and worked for Rowan Yarns as a Design Consultant – which is where she met Donna. 'Elements' will be Alison's fourth knitting book, and her first collaborative project. Like Donna, she is a passionate and committed knitting teacher, and has taught workshops for over ten years.

Her knitting focuses on detailed, often delicate designs with the emphasis on accessories and an occasional foray into home-ware knitting. Perhaps best known for a career-long love affair with Rowan's Kidsilk Haze and beads, her preferred territory covers texture, subtle colour-ways and elegant knits.

Alison lives and works in Somerset, England and can be found at www.alisoncrowthersmith.com.

"I am a very literal designer. When I see pleasing images, especially shapes, my mind instantly begins to try and recreate something of that imagery, in a knitted design. Once I know what I want to knit, I work backwards and layer the design elements into it. My focus tends to be on detailed features, such as a tailored cuff or a decorative texture, which I hope add elegance and a sense of the 'whole', as well as being really pleasing to knit.

"Because I break my design process down into these layers, often the overall impression may be of an intricate, even difficult knit; but in fact, if I have a trade-mark I think it would be that each element of my designs is not very difficult, but added together, they look as if they were. One of my aims is to make you, the knitter, feel amazing.

"I also like fairly small or medium-sized projects, because I am a big fan of completing my knitting within a reasonable timescale, or at least within my tolerance for boredom, which is fairly generous – but not boundless.

"Working on 'Elements' has enabled me to draw upon my own land, here in Somerset. This large and beautiful county is full of vivid contrasts and atmospheric landscapes, some of which are reflected in my designs."

JONES

Donna Jones was taught to knit when she was 4 years old by her mother and has been surrounded by yarn for as long as she can remember. She has also worked as a Design Consultant and freelance tutor for Rowan Yarns, and continues to teach a broad range of topics to equip participants with the skills they need, as well as encouraging their creativity.

Donna's style is warmly rustic, reflecting a deep love of nature, colour and quirky detail. Her designs and yarn preferences express an appreciation of functional and comforting knitting, with intriguing structural elements or decorative touches.

Donna lives and works in South Wales, sharing a home with her musician husband and a very pampered cat. She can be found at www.fyberknitics.co.uk

"Although I love texture I think I'm primarily driven by colour in my creative work. I never cease to be fascinated by how colours are altered when placed next to others - I am always on the lookout for interesting and exciting colour combinations.

"Sometimes ideas will form fairly quickly, but more often than not I'm a slow burner, ruminating on ideas and images for some time before I develop these. I find inspiration for designs in many different ways and my design process will vary accordingly. Sometimes starting with a particular stitch, detail or technique that I find interesting and then develop into a design, and then at other times starting with a particular design in mind and choosing the stitches,

techniques and materials that best express that idea. In both scenarios though, I would say that the ideas, or refinement of ideas come from playing around with the materials and a sketch book.

"Allowing yourself time to play (and make mistakes) is an essential part of any creative work, and ideas are more likely to flow when you give yourself permission to simply explore rather than 'produce'. I believe that creativity is like a muscle that needs to be used regularly – we all have an ability to be creative, and it's good for you!"